Matthew Arnold

**Last essays on church and religion**

Matthew Arnold

**Last essays on church and religion**

ISBN/EAN: 9783743301344

Manufactured in Europe, USA, Canada, Australia, Japa

Cover: Foto ©Thomas Meinert / pixelio.de

Manufactured and distributed by brebook publishing software
(www.brebook.com)

Matthew Arnold

**Last essays on church and religion**

# LAST ESSAYS

## ON

# CHURCH AND RELIGION

BY

## MATTHEW ARNOLD

FORMERLY PROFESSOR OF POETRY IN THE UNIVERSITY OF OXFORD
AND FELLOW OF ORIEL COLLEGE

LONDON

SMITH, ELDER, & CO., 15 WATERLOO PLACE

1877

# PREFACE.

THE PRESENT VOLUME closes the series of my attempts
to deal directly with questions concerning religion and
the Church.  Indirectly such questions must often, in
all serious literary work, present themselves ; but in
this volume I make them my direct object for the last
time.  Assuredly it was not for my own pleasure that
I entered upon them at first, and it is with anything
but reluctance that I now part from them.  Neither can
I be ignorant what offence my handling of them has
given to many whose good-will I value, and with what
relief they will learn that the handling is now to
cease.  Personal considerations, however, ought not in
a matter like this to bear sway ; and they have not,
in fact, determined me to bring to an end the work
which I had been pursuing.  But the thing which I
proposed to myself to do has, so far as my powers

enabled me to do it, been done. What I wished to
say has been said. And in returning to devote to
literature, more strictly so-called, what remains to me
of life and strength and leisure, I am returning, after
all, to a field where work of the most important kind
has now to be done, though indirectly, for religion. I
am persuaded that the transformation of religion, which
is essential for its perpetuance, can be accomplished only
by carrying the qualities of flexibility, perceptiveness, and
judgment, which are the best fruits of letters, to whole
classes of the community which now know next to nothing of them, and by procuring the application of those
qualities to matters where they are never applied now.

A survey of the forms and tendencies which religion exhibits at the present day in England has been
made lately by a man of genius, energy, and sympathy,
—Mr. Gladstone. Mr. Gladstone seems disposed to fix
as the test of value, for those several forms, their
greater or lesser adaptedness to the mind of masses of
our people. It may be admitted that religion ought
to be capable of reaching the mind of masses of men.
It may be admitted that a religion not plain and
simple, a religion of abstractions and intellectual refinements, cannot influence masses of men. But it

is an error to imagine that the mind of our masses, or even the mind of our religious world, is something which may remain just as it now is, and that religion will have to adapt itself to that mind just as it now is. At least as much change is required, and will have to take place, in that mind as in religion. Gross of perception and materialising that mind is, at present, still disposed to be. Yet at the same time it is undeniable that the old anthropomorphic and miraculous religion, suited in many respects to such a mind, no longer reaches and rules it as it once did. A check and disturbance to religion thence arises. But let us impute the disturbance to the right cause. It is not to be imputed merely to the inadequacy of the old materialising religion, and to be remedied by giving to this religion a form still materialising, but more acceptable. It is to be imputed, in at least an equal degree, to the grossness of perception and materialising habits of the popular mind, which unfit it for any religion not lending itself, like the old popular religion, to those habits ; while yet, from other causes, that old religion cannot maintain its sway. And it is to be remedied by a gradual transformation of the popular mind, by slowly curing it of its grossness of perception and of its materialising habits, not by keeping religion materialistic that it may correspond to them.

The conditions of the religious question are, in truth, profoundly misapprehended in this country. In England and in America religion has retained so much hold upon the affections of the community, that the partisans of popular religion are easily led to entertain illusions; to fancy that the difficulties of their case are much less than they are, that they can make terms which they cannot make, and save things which they cannot save. A good medicine for such illusions would be the perusal of the criticisms which *Literature and Dogma* has encountered on the Continent. Here in England that book passes, in general, for a book revolutionary and anti-religious. In foreign critics of the liberal school it provokes a feeling of mingled astonishment and impatience; impatience, that religion should be set on new grounds when they had hoped that religion, the old ground having in the judgment of all rational persons given way, was going to ruin as fast as could fairly be expected; astonishment, that any man of liberal tendencies should not agree with them.

Particularly striking, in this respect, were the remarks upon *Literature and Dogma* of M. Challemel-Lacour, in France, and of Professor de Gubernatis, in Italy. Professor de Gubernatis is perhaps the most accomplished man in Italy ; he is certainly one of the most intelligent. M. Challemel-Lacour is, or was, one of the best, gravest, most deeply interesting and instructive, of French writers. His admirable series of articles on Wilhelm von Humboldt, which I read a good many years ago in the *Revue des Deux Mondes*, still live as fresh in my memory as if I had read them yesterday. M. Challemel-Lacour has become an ardent politician. It is well known how politics, in France, govern men's treatment of the religious question. Some little temper and heat are excusable, undoubtedly, when religion raises in a man's mind simply the image of the clerical party and of his sworn political foes. Perhaps a man's view of religion, however, must necessarily in this case be somewhat warped. Professor de Gubernatis is not a politician ; he is an independent friend of progress, of high studies, and of intelligence. His remarks on *Literature and Dogma*, therefore, and on the attempt made in that book to give a new life to religion by giving a new sense to words of the Bible, have even a greater significance than M. Challemel-

Lacour's.   For Italy and for Italians, says Professor de
Gubernatis, such an attempt has and can have no interest
whatever.   'In Italy the Bible is just this :—for priests,
a sacred text ; for infidels, a book full of obscurities
and contradictions ; for the learned, an historical document to be used with great caution ; for lovers of literature, a collection of very fine specimens of Oriental poetic
eloquence.   But it never has been, and never will be,
a fruitful inspirer of men's daily life.'   'And how wonderful,' Professor de Gubernatis adds, 'that anyone
should wish to make it so, and should raise intellectual
and literary discussions having this for their object !'
'It is strange that the human genius should take
pleasure in combating in such narrow lists, with such
treacherous ground under one's feet, with such a cloudy
sky over one's head ;—and all this in the name of freedom
of discussion!'   'What would the author of *Literature
and Dogma* say,' concludes Professor de Gubernatis,
'if Plato had based his republic upon a text of
Hesiod ;—*se Platone avesse fondata la sua Repubblica
sopra un testo d'Esiodo?*'   That is to say, the Bible
has no more solidity and value, as a basis for human
life, than the *Theogony.*

Here we have, undoubtedly, the genuine opinion of

Continental liberalism concerning the religion of the Bible
and its future.   It is stated with unusual frankness and
clearness, but it is the genuine opinion.   It is not an
opinion which at present prevails at all widely either in
this countiy or in America.   But when we consider the
immense change which, in other matters where tradition
and convention were the obstacles to change, has befallen
the thought of this country since the Continent was opened
at the end of the great war, we cannot doubt that in
religion, too, the mere barriers of tradition and convention will finally give way, that a common European
level of thought will establish itself, and will spread to
America also.   Of course there will be backwaters,
more or less strong, of superstition and obscurantism ; but
I speak of the probable development of opinion in those
classes which are to be called progressive and liberal.
Such classes are undoubtedly the multiplying and prevailing body both here and in America.   And I say that,
if we judge the future from the past, these classes, in any
matter where it is tradition and convention that at
present isolates them from the common liberal opinion
of Europe, will, with time, be drawn almost inevitably
into that opinion.

The partisans of traditional religion in this country

do not know, I think, how decisively the whole force of
progressive and liberal opinion on the Continent has
pronounced against the Christian religion.   They do
not know how surely the whole force of progressive
and liberal opinion in this country tends to follow, so
far as traditional religion is concerned, the opinion of
the Continent.   They dream of patching up things un-
mendable, of retaining what can never be retained, of
stopping change at a point where it can never be stopped.
The undoubted tendency of liberal opinion is to reject
the whole anthropomorphic and miraculous religion of
tradition, as unsound and untenable.   On the Continent
such opinion has rejected it already.   One cannot blame
the rejection.   'Things are what they are,' and the
religion of tradition, Catholic or Protestant, _is_ unsound
and untenable.   A greater force of tradition in favour of
religion is all which now prevents the liberal opinion in
this country from following Continental opinion.   That
force is not of a nature to be permanent, and it will not, in
fact, hold out long.   But a very grave question is behind.

Rejecting, henceforth, all concern with the obsolete
religion of tradition, the liberalism of the Continent
rejects also, and on the like grounds, all concern with
the Bible and Christianity.   To claim for the Bible the

direction, in any way, of modern life, is, we hear, as if
Plato had sought to found his ideal republic 'upon a text
of Hesiod.' The real question is whether this conclusion, too, of modern liberalism is to be admitted, like
the conclusion that traditionary religion is unsound and
obsolete. And it does not find many gainsayers. Ob-
scurantists are glad to see the question placed on this
footing : that the cause of traditionary religion, and the
cause of Christianity in general, must stand or fall together. For they see but very little way into the future ;
and in the immediate present this way of putting the
question tells, as they clearly perceive, in their favour.
In the immediate present many will be tempted to cling
to the traditionary religion with their eyes shut, rather
than accept the extinction of Christianity. Other friends
of religion are busy with fantastic projects, which can
never come to anything, but which prevent their seeing
the real character of the situation. So the thesis of
modern liberals on the Continent, that Christianity in
general stands on the same footing as traditionary religion and must share its fate, meets with little direct
discussion or opposition. And liberal opinion everywhere will at last grow accustomed to finding that
thesis put forward as certain, will become familiarised

with it, will suppose that no one disputes it. This in itself will tend to withhold men from any serious return upon their own minds in the matter. Meanwhile the day will most certainly arrive, when the great body of liberal opinion in this country will adhere to the first half of the doctrine of Continental liberals ;—will admit that traditionary religion is utterly untenable. And the danger is, that from the habits of their minds, and from seeing the thing treated as certain, and from hearing nothing urged against it, our liberals may admit as indisputable the second half of the doctrine too : that Christianity, also, is untenable.

And therefore is it so all-important to insist on what I call the *natural truth* of Christianity, and to bring this out all we can. Liberal opinion tends, as we have seen, to treat traditional religion and Christianity as identical ; if one is unsound, so is the other. Especially, however, does liberal opinion show this tendency among the Latin nations, on whom Protestantism did not lay hold ; and it shows it most among those Latin nations of whom Protestantism laid hold least, such as Italy and Spain. For Protestantism was undoubtedly, whatever may have been its faults and miscarriages, an assertion of the natural truth of Christianity for the mind and con-

science of men. The question is, whether Christianity
has this natural truth or not.   It is a question of fact.
In the end the victory belongs to facts, and he who
contradicts them finds that he runs his head against a
wall.   Our traditional religion turns out not to have,
in fact, natural truth, the only truth which can stand.
The miracles of our traditional religion, like other
miracles, did not happen ; its metaphysical proofs of God
are mere words.   Has or has not Christianity, in fact, the
same want of natural truth as our traditional religion ?   It
is a question of immense importance.   Of questions
about religion, it may be said to be at the present time,
for a serious man, the only important one.

Now, whoever seeks to show the natural truth of a
thing which professes to be for general use, ought to try
to be as simple as possible.   He ought not to allow himself to have any recourse either to intellectual refinements or to sentimental rhetoric.   And therefore it is
well to start, in bringing out the truth of Christianity,
with a plain proposition such as everybody, one would
think, must admit: the proposition that conduct is a
very important matter.   I have called conduct three-
fourths of life.   M. Challemel-Lacour quarrels greatly
with the proposition.   Certainly people in general do not

a

behave as if they were convinced that conduct is three-
fourths of life. Butler well says that even religious people
are always for placing the stress of their religion anywhere
other than on virtue ;—virtue being simply the good
direction of conduct. We know, too, that the Italians
at the Renascence changed the very meaning of the
word virtue altogether, and made their *virtù* mean a
love of the fine arts and of intellectual culture. And we
see the fruits of the new definition in the Italy of the
seventeenth and eighteenth centuries. We will not,
then, there being all this opposition, offer to settle the
exact proportion of life which conduct may be said to
be. But that conduct is, at any rate, a very considerable part of life, will generally be admitted.

It will generally be admitted, too, that all experience
as to conduct brings us at last to the fact of two selves,
or instincts, or forces,—name them how we will, and however we may suppose them to have arisen,—contending
for the mastery in man : one, a movement of first impulse
and more involuntary, leading us to gratify any inclination
that may solicit us, and called generally a movement of
man's ordinary or passing self, of sense, appetite, desire ;
the other, a movement of reflexion and more voluntary,
leading us to submit inclination to some rule, and called

generally a movement of man's higher or enduring self, of reason, spirit, will. The thing is described in different words by different nations and men relating their experience of it, but as to the thing itself they all, or all the most serious and important among them, agree. This, I think, will be admitted. Nor will it be denied that they all come to the conclusion that for a man to obey the higher self, or reason, or whatever it is to be called, is happiness and life for him ; to obey the lower is death and misery. It will be allowed, again, that whatever men's minds are to fasten and rest upon, whatever is to hold their attention and to rule their practice, naturally embodies itself for them in certain examples, precepts, and sayings, to which they perpetually recur. Without a frame or body of this kind, a set of thoughts cannot abide with men and sustain them. 'If ye abide in me,' says Jesus, ' ye shall know the truth, and the truth shall make you free ; '—not if you keep skipping about all over the world for various renderings of it. ' It behoves us to know,' says Epictetus, ' that a principle can hardly establish itself with a man, unless he every day utters the same things, hears the same things, and applies them withal to his life.' And naturally the body of examples and precepts, which men should use for this purpose, ought to be those which most impressively represent the principle, or the set of thoughts, commending itself to their minds for respect and attention. And the more the precepts are used, the more will men's sentiments cluster around them, and the more dear and solemn will they be.

Now to apply this to Christianity. It is evident that to what they called *righteousness,*—a name which covers all that we mean by conduct,—the Jewish nation attached pre-eminent, unique importance. This impassioned testimony of theirs to the weight of a thing admittedly of very considerable importance, has its own value of a special kind. But it is well known how imperfectly and amiss the Jewish nation conceived righteousness. And finally, when their misconceived righteousness failed them in actual life more and more, they took refuge in imaginings about the future, and filled themselves with hopes of a *kingdom of God,* a *resurrection,* a *judgment,* an *eternal life,* bringing in and establishing for ever this misconceived righteousness of theirs. As God's agent in this work of restoring the kingdom to Israel they promised to themselves an Anointed and Chosen One, *Christ the son of God.*[1]

[1] John, xx, 31.

Jesus Christ found, when he came among his countrymen, all these phrases and ideas ruling their minds.  Conduct or righteousness, a matter admittedly of very considerable importance, and which the Jews thought of paramount importance, they had come entirely to misconceive, and had created an immense poetry of hopes and imaginings in favour of their misconception.  What did Jesus do?  From his countrymen's errors about righteousness he reverted to the solid, authentic, universal fact of experience about it : the fact of the higher and lower self in man, inheritors the one of them of happiness, the other of misery.  He possessed himself of it, he made it the centre of his teaching.  He made it so in the well-known formula, his *secret* : 'He that will save his life shall lose it ; he that do love his life shall save it.'  And by his admirable figure of the *two lives* of man, the real life and the seeming life, he connected this profound fact of experience with that attractive poetry of hopes and imaginings which possessed the minds of his countrymen.  Eternal life?  Yes, the life in the higher and undying self of man.  Judgment?  Yes, the trying, in conscience, of the claims and instigations of the two lives, and the decision between them.  Resurrection?  Yes, the rising from bondage and tran-

sience with the lower life to victory and permanence
with the higher. The kingdom of God? Yes, the reign
amongst mankind of the higher life. The Christ the son
of God? Yes, the bringer-in and founder of this reign
of the higher life, this true kingdom of God.

But we can go farther. Observers say, with much
appearance of truth, that all our passions may be run up
into two elementary instincts : the reproductive instinct
and the instinct of self-preservation. It is evident to
what these instincts will in themselves carry the man
who follows the lower self of sense, and appetite, and first
impulse. It is evident, also, that they are directly con-
trolled by two forces which Christianity,—following that
law of the higher life which St. Paul names indifferently
the *law of God*, the *law of our mind*, the *line of thought
of the spirit*[1]—has set up as its two grand virtues : kindness and pureness, charity and chastity. If any virtues
could stand for the whole of Christianity, these might.
Let us have them from the mouth of Jesus Christ himself.
' He that loveth his life shall lose it ; a new commandment give I unto you that ye love *one another.*' There is
charity. ' Blest are the pure in heart, for they shall see
God.' There is purity.

[1] φοόνημα τοῦ πνεύματος.

We go here simply on experience, having to establish the *natural truth* of Christianity. That the 'new commandment' of charity is enjoined by the Bible, gives it therefore, we shall suppose, no force at all, unless it turns out to be enjoined also by experience. And it is enjoined by experience if experience shows that it is necessary to human happiness,—that men cannot get on without it. Now really if there is a lesson which in our day has come to force itself upon everybody, in all quarters and by all channels, it is the lesson of the *solidarity* as it is called by modern philosophers, of men. If there was ever a notion tempting to common human nature, it was the notion that the rule of 'every man for himself' was the rule of happiness. But at last it turns out as a matter of experience, and so plainly that it is coming to be even generally admitted,—it turns out that the only real happiness is in a kind of impersonal higher life, where the happiness of others counts with a man as essential to his own. He that loves his life does really turn out to lose it, and the new commandment proves its own truth by experience.

And the other great Christian virtue, pureness? Here the case is somewhat different. One hears doubts raised, nowadays, as to the natural truth of this virtue.

While science has adopted, as a truth confirmed by experience, the Christian idea of charity, long supposed to
conflict with experience, and has decked it out with the
grand title of *human solidarity*, one may hear many doubts
thrown, in the name of science and reason, on the truth
and validity of the Christian idea of pureness.    As
a mere *commandment* this virtue cannot have the
authority which it once had, for the notion of *commandments* in this sense is giving way.    And on its natural
truth, when the thing comes to be tested by experience,
doubts are thrown.    Well, experience must decide.    It is
a question of fact.    'There is no honest woman who is
not sick of her trade,' says La Rochefoucauld.    'I pass
for having enjoyed life,' said Ninon in old age, 'but if
anyone had told me beforehand what my life was going
to be I would have hanged myself.'    Who is right?    On
which side is *natural truth*?    It will be admitted that
there can hardly be a more vital question for human
society.    And those who doubt on which side is natural
truth, and who raise the question, will have to learn by
experience.    But finely touched souls have a presentiment of a thing's natural truth even though it be ques-
tioned, and long before the palpable proof by experience
convinces all the world.    They have it quite indepen-

dently of their attitude towards traditional religion. 'May the idea of *pureness*, extending itself to the very morsel which I take into my mouth, grow ever clearer in me and clearer!'[1] So prayed Goethe. And all such well-inspired souls will perceive the profound natural truth of the idea of pureness, and will be sure, therefore, that the more boldly it is challenged, the more sharply and signally will experience mark its truth. So that of the two great Christian virtues, charity and chastity, kindness and pureness, the one has at this moment the most signal testimony from experience to its intrinsic truth and weight, and the other is expecting it.

All this may enable us to understand how admirably fitted are Jesus Christ and his precepts to serve as mankind's standing reminder as to conduct,—to serve as men's religion. Jesus Christ and his precepts are found to hit the moral experience of mankind, to hit it in the critical points, to hit it lastingly; and, when doubts are thrown upon their really hitting it, then to come out stronger than ever. And we know how Jesus Christ and his precepts won their way from the very first, and soon became the religion of all that part of the world which

---

[1] 'Möge die Idee des *Reinen*, die sich auf den Bissen erstreckt den ich in den Mund nehme, immer lichter in mir werden!'

most counted, and are now the religion of all that part of the world which most counts. This they certainly in great part owed, even from the first, to that instinctive sense of their natural fitness for such a service, of their natural truth and weight, which amidst all misapprehensions of them they inspired.

Moreover, we must always keep in sight one specially important element in the power exercised by Jesus Christ and his precepts. And that is, the impression left by Jesus of what we call *sweet reason* in the highest degree; of consummate justness in what he said, perfect balance, unerring felicity. For this impression has been a great element of progress. It made half the charm of the religion of Jesus in the first instance, and it makes it still. But it also serves in an admirable way against the misapprehensions with which men received, as we have said, and could not but receive, the natural truth he gave them, and which they made up along with that truth into their religion. For it is felt that anything exaggerated, distorted, false, cannot be from Jesus ; that it must be human perversion of him. There is always an appeal open, and a return possible, to the acknowledged sweet reason of Jesus, to his 'grace and truth.' And thus Christians, instead of sticking for ever because of their religion to errors which they themselves have put into their religion, find in their religion itself a ground for breaking with them. For example : medieval charity and medieval chastity are manifestly misgrowths, however natural,—misgrowths unworkable and dangerous,—of the ideas of kindness and pureness. Then they cannot have come from Jesus; they cannot be what Jesus meant. Such is the inevitable inference ; and Christianity here touches a spring for self-correction and self-readjustment which is of the highest value.

And, finally, the figure and sayings of Jesus, embodying and representing men's moral experience to them, serving them as a perpetual reminder of it, by a fixed form of words and observances holding their attention to it, and thus attaching them, have attracted to themselves, by the very force of time, and use, and association, a mass of additional attachment, and a host of sentiments the most tender and profound.

This, then, is what we mean by saying that Christianity has natural truth. By this truth things must stand, not by people's wishes and asseverations about them. *Omnium Deus est, cujus, velimus aut nolimus, omnes sumus,* says Tertullian. 'The God of all of us is the God that we all belong to whether we will or no.' The

Eternal that makes for righteousness is such a God ; and
he is the God of Christianity.    Jesus explains what this
God would have of us ; and the strength of Jesus is that
he explains it right.    The natural experimental truth of
√ his explanations is their one claim upon us ; but this is
claim enough.    Does the thing, being admittedly most
important, turn out to be as he says ?  If it does, then we
' belong to him whether we will or no.'

A recent German writer, wishing to exalt Schopenhauer at the expense of Jesus, says that both Jesus and
Schopenhauer taught the true doctrine of self-renouncement, but that Schopenhauer faced the pessimism which
is that doctrine's natural accompaniment, whereas Jesus
sought to escape from it by the dream of a paradise to
come.    This critic credits Jesus, as usual, with the
very misconceptions against which he strove.    It was
the effort of Jesus to place the bliss, the eternal life of
popular religion, not where popular religion placed
it, in a fantastic paradise to come, but in the joy of self-
renouncement.    This was the 'eternal life' of Jesus ;
this was his 'joy;'—the joy which he desired that his
disciples, too, might have full and complete, might
have ' fulfilled in themselves.'    His depth, his truth, his
rightness, come out in this very point : that he saw that

self-renouncement *is* joy, and that human life, in which it takes place, is therefore a blessing and a benefit. And just exactly here is his superiority to Schopenhauer. Jesus hits the plain natural truth that human life is a blessing and a benefit, while Schopenhauer misses it. ' It is evident, even *a priori*, that the world is doomed to evil, and that it is the domain of irrationality. In abstinence from the further propagation of mankind is salvation. This would gradually bring about the extinction of our species, and, with our extinction, that of the universe, since the universe requires for its existence the co-operation of human thought.' The fault of this sort of thing is, that it is plainly, somehow or other, a paradox, and that human thought (I say it with due deference to the many persons for whom Schopenhauer is just now in fashion) instinctively feels it to be absurd. The *fact* is with Jesus. ' The Eternal is king, the earth may be *glad* thereof.' Human life is a blessing and a benefit, and constantly improvable, because in self-renouncement is a fount of joy, 'springing up unto everlasting life.' Not only, ' It is more *right* to give than to receive,' more rational, more necessary; but, ' It is more *blessed* to give than to receive.'

The *fact*, I say, the real *fact*, is what it imports us

to reach.  A writer of remarkable knowledge, judgment,
and impartiality, M. Maurice Vernes, of the *Revue Scienti-
fique*, objects to the contrast of an earlier intuition of
Israel, *Righteousness tendeth to life, the righteous is an
everlasting foundation*, with a later ' Aberglaube,' such as
we find in the Book of Daniel, and such as Jesus had
to deal with.   He objects to the contrast of the doctrine
of Jesus with the metaphysics of the Church.   M. Maurice Vernes is one of those, of whom  there are so many,
who  have  a  philosophical system  of history,—a history
ruled by the law of progress, of evolution.   Between the
eighth century before our era and the  second, the law of
evolution  must have  been at work.   Progress must have
gone on.   Therefore the Messianic ideas of the  Book of
Daniel must be  a  higher stage than  the ideas of  the
great prophets and wise men of  the eighth and  ninth
centuries.   Again.   The importation of metaphysics into
Christianity means the arrival of Greek thought, Western
thought,—the enrichment of the early Christian thought
with new elements.    This is evolution, development.
And therefore, apparently, the Athanasian Creed must
be a higher stage than the Sermon on the Mount.

Let us salute with respect that imposing generality,
the law of evolution.   But let us remember that, in each

particular case which comes before us, what concerns us is, surely, the *fact* as to that particular case. And surely, as a matter of fact, the ideas of the great prophets and wise men of the eighth or ninth century before Christ are profounder and more true than the ideas of the eschatologist of the Book of Daniel. As a matter of fact, again, the ideas of Jesus in the Sermon on the Mount are surely profounder and more true than the ideas of the theologian of the Athanasian Creed. Ins and outs of this kind may settle their business with the general law of evolution as they can; but our business is with the fact. And the fact, surely, is here as we have stated it.

M. Vernes further objects to our picking and choosing among the records of Jesus, and pronouncing that whatever suits us shall be held to come from Jesus, and whatever does not suit us from his reporters. But here, again, it is a question of fact ;—a question, which of two things is, in fact, more likely? Is it, in fact, more likely that Jesus, being what we can see from certain of the data about him that he was, should have been in many points misunderstood and misrepresented by his followers ; or that, being what by those data he was, he should also have been at the same time the thaumatur-

gical personage that his followers imagined? The more
reasonable Jesus is likewise, surely, the more real one.

I believe, then, that the real God, the real Jesus, will
continue to command allegiance, because we do, in fact,
'belong to them.' I believe that Christianity will survive
because of its natural truth. Those who fancied that they
had done with it, those who had thrown it aside because
what was presented to them under its name was so unre-
ceivable, will have to return to it again, and to learn it
better. The Latin nations,—even the southern Latin
nations,—will have to acquaint themselves with that
fundamental document of Christianity, the Bible, and to
discover wherein it differs from 'a text of Hesiod.' Neither will the old forms of Christian worship be extin-
guished by the growth of a truer conception of their
essential contents. Those forms, thrown out at dimly-
grasped truth, approximative and provisional represen-
tations of it, and which are now surrounded with such an
atmosphere of tender and profound sentiment, will not disappear. They will survive as poetry. Above all, among
the Catholic nations will this be the case. And, indeed,
one must wonder at the fatuity of the Roman Catholic
Church, that she should not herself see what a future
there is for her here. Will there never arise among

Catholics some great soul, to perceive that the eternity and universality, which is vainly claimed for Catholic dogma and the ultramontane system, might really be possible for Catholic worship? But to rule over the moment and the credulous has more attraction than to work for the future and the sane.

Christianity, however, will find the ways for its own future. What is certain is that it will not disappear. Whatever progress may be made in science, art, and literary culture,—however much higher, more general, and more effective than at present the value for them may become,--Christianity will be still there as what these rest against and imply; as the indispensable background, ᵥ the *three-fourths of life.* It is true, while the remaining fourth is ill-cared for, the three-fourths themselves must also suffer with it. But this does but bring us to the old and true Socratic thesis of the interdependence of virtue and knowledge. And we cannot, then, do better than conclude with some excellent words of Mr. Jowett, doing homage, in the preface introducing his translation of Plato's Protagoras, to that famous thesis. 'This is an aspect of the truth which was lost almost as soon as it was found; and yet has to be recovered by every

b

one for himself who would pass the limits of proverbial and popular philosophy. The moral and intellectual are always dividing, yet they must be reunited, and in the highest conception of them are inseparable.'

# CONTENTS.

WHOEVER has to impugn the soundness of popular theology will most certainly find parts in his task which are
unwelcome and painful. Other parts in it, however, are
full of reward. And none more so than those, in which
the work to be done is positive, not negative, and uniting, not dividing ; in which what survives in Christianity
is dwelt upon, not what perishes ; and what offers us
points of contact with the religion of the community,
rather than motives for breaking with it. Popular religion is too forward to employ arguments which may well
be called arguments of despair. 'Take me in the lump,' it
cries, ' or give up Christianity altogether. Construe the
Bible as I do, or renounce my public worship and solem-
nities ; renounce all communion with me, as an imposture
and falsehood on your part. Quit, as weak-minded,
deluded blunderers, all those doctors and lights of the
Church who have long served you, aided you, been dear
to you. Those teachers set forth what are, in your
opinion, errors, and go on grounds which you believe to

B

be hollow. Whoever thinks as you do, ought, if he is courageous and consistent, to trust such blind guides no more, but to remain staunch by his new lights and himself.'

It happens, I suppose, to most people who treat an interesting subject, and it happens to me, to receive from those whom the subject interests, and who may have in general followed one's treatment of it with sympathy, avowals of difficulty upon certain points, requests for explanation. But the discussion of a subject, more especially of a religious subject, may easily be pursued longer than is advisable. On the immense difference which there seems to me to be between the popular conception of Christianity and the true conception of it, I have said what I wished to say. I wished to say it, partly in order to aid those whom the popular conception embarrassed; partly because, having frequently occasion to assert the truth and importance of Christianity against those who disparaged them, I was bound in honesty to make clear what sort of Christianity I meant. But having said, however imperfectly, what I wished, I leave, and am glad to leave, a discussion where the hope to do good must always be mixed with an apprehension of doing harm. Only, in leaving it, I will conclude with what cannot, one may hope, do harm : an endeavour to dispel some difficulties raised by the *arguments of despair*, as I have called them, of popular religion.

I have formerly spoken at much length of the writings of St. Paul, pointing out what a clue he gives us to the right understanding of the word *resurrection*, the great word of Christianity; and how he deserves, on this account, our special interest and study. It is the *spiritual* resurrection of which he is thus the instructive expounder to us. But undoubtedly he believed also in the miracle of the physical resurrection, both of Jesus himself and for mankind at large. This belief those who do not admit the miraculous will not share with him. And one who does not admit the miraculous, but who yet had continued to think St. Paul worthy of all honour and his teaching full of instruction, brings forward to me a sentence from an eloquent and most popular author, wherein it is said that 'St. Paul—surely no imbecile or credulous enthusiast—vouches for the reality of the (physical) resurrection, of the appearances of Jesus after it, and of his own vision. Must then St. Paul, he asks, if he was mistaken in thus vouching,—which whoever does not admit the miraculous cannot but suppose,—of necessity be an ' imbecile and credulous enthusiast,' and his words and character of no more value to us than those of that slight sort of people? And again, my questioner finds the same author saying, that to suppose St. Paul and the Evangelists mistaken about the miracles which they allege, is to ' insinuate that the faith of Christendom was founded on most facile and reprehensible credulity, and this in men who have taught the spirit of truthfulness as a primary duty of the religion which they preached.' And he inquires whether St. Paul and the Evangelists, in admitting the miraculous, were really founding the faith of Christendom on most facile and reprehensible credulity, and were false to the spirit of truthfulness taught by themselves as the primary duty of the religion which they preached.

Let me answer by putting a parallel case. The argument is that St. Paul, by believing and asserting the reality of the physical resurrection and subsequent appearances of Jesus, proves himself, supposing those alleged facts not to have happened, an imbecile or credulous enthusiast, and an unprofitable guide. St. Paul's vision we need not take into account, because even those who do not admit the miraculous will readily admit that he had his vision, only they say it is to be explained naturally. But they do not admit the reality of the physical resurrection of Jesus and of his appearances afterwards, while yet they must own that St. Paul did. The question is, does either the belief of these things by a man of signal truthfulness, judgment, and mental power in St. Paul's circumstances, prove them to have really happened ; or does his believing them, in spite of their not having really happened, prove that he cannot have been a man of great truthfulness, judgment, and mental power?

Undeniably St. Paul was mistaken about the imminence of the end of the world. But this was a matter of expectation, not experience. If he was mistaken about a grave fact alleged to have already positively happened, such as the bodily resurrection of Jesus, he must, it is argued, have been a credulous and imbecile enthusiast.

2.

I have already mentioned elsewhere [1] Sir Matthew Hale's belief in the reality of witchcraft. The contemporary records of this belief in our own country and among our own people, in a century of great intellectual force and achievement, and when the printing press fixed and preserved the accounts of public proceedings to which the charge of witchcraft gave rise, are of extraordinary interest. They throw an invaluable light for us on the history of the human spirit. I think it is not an illusion of national self-esteem to flatter ourselves that something of the English 'good nature and good humour'

[1] *God and the Bible*, p. 387.

is not absent even from these repulsive records ; that
from the traits of infuriated, infernal cruelty which characterise similar records elsewhere, particularly among the
Latin nations, they are in a great measure free. They
reveal, too, beginnings of that revolt of good sense,
gleams of that reason, that criticism, which was presently
to disperse the long-prevailing belief in witchcraft. At
the beginning of the eighteenth century Addison, though
he himself looks with disfavour on a man who wholly dis-
believes in ghosts and apparitions, yet smiles at Sir
Roger De Coverley's belief in witches, as a belief which
intelligent men had outgrown, a survival from times of
ignorance. Nevertheless, in 1716, two women were
hanged at Huntingdon for witchcraft. But they were the
last victims, and in 1736 the penal statutes against
witchcraft were repealed. And by the end of the eighteenth century, the majority of rational people had come
to disbelieve, not in witches only, but in ghosts also.
Incredulity had become the rule, credulity the exception.

But through the greater part of the seventeenth
century things were just the other way. Credulity
about witchcraft was the rule, incredulity the exception.
It is by its all-pervadingness, its seemingly inevitable and
natural character, that this credulity of the seventeenth
century is distinguished from modern growths which are

sometimes compared with it. In the addiction to what
is called spiritualism, there is something factitious and
artificial. It is quite easy to pay no attention to spiri-
tu. sts and their exhibitions ; and a man of serious
er, a man even of matured sense, will in general pay
none. He will instinctively apply Goethe's excellent
caution : that we have all of us a nervous system which
can easily be worked upon, that we are most of us very
easily puzzled, and that it is foolish, by idly perplexing
our understanding and playing with our nervous system,
to titillate in ourselves the fibre of superstition. Whoever runs after our modern sorcerers may indeed find
them. He may make acquaintance with their new spiritual visitants who have succeeded to the old-fashioned
imps of the seventeenth century,—to the Jarmara, Ele-
mauzer, Sack and Sugar, Vinegar Tom, and Grizzel
Greedigut, of our trials for witchcraft. But he may also
pass his life without troubling his head about them and
their masters. In the seventeenth century, on the other
hand, the belief in witches and their works met a man at
every turn, and created an atmosphere for his thoughts
which they could not help feeling. A man who scouted
the belief, who even disparaged it, was called Sadducee,
atheist, and infidel. Relations of the conviction of
witches had their sharp word of ‘ condemnation for the

particular opinion of some men who suppose there be
none at all.' They had their caution to him 'to take
heed how he either despised the power of God in his
creatures, or vilipended the subtlety and fury of the Devil
as God's minister of vengeance.' The ministers of religion took a leading part in the proceedings against
witches ; the Puritan ministers were here particularly
busy. Scripture had said : *Thou shalt not suffer a witch
to live.* And, strange to say, the poor creatures tried and
executed for witchcraft appear to have usually been themselves firm believers in their own magic. They confess
their compact with the Devil, and specify the imps, or
familiars, whom they have at their disposal. All this, I
say, created for the mind an atmosphere from which it
was hard to escape. Again and again we hear of the
'sufficient justices of the peace and discreet magistrates,'
of the 'persons of great knowledge,' who were satisfied
with the proofs of witchcraft offered to them. It is abundantly clear that to take as solid and convincing, where
a witch was in question, evidence which would now be
accepted by no reasonable man, was in the seventeenth
century quite compatible with truthfulness of disposition,
vigour of intelligence, and penetrating judgment on other
matters.

Certainly these three advantages,—truthfulness of dis-

position, vigour of intelligence, and penetrating judgment,—were possessed in a signal degree by the famous
Chief Justice of Charles the Second's reign, Sir Matthew
Hale. Burnet notices the remarkable mixture in him
of sweetness with gravity, so to the three fore-named
advantages we may add gentleness of temper. There is
extant the report of a famous trial for witchcraft before
Sir Matthew Hale.[1] Two widows of Lowestoft in Suffolk,
named Rose Cullender and Amy Duny, were tried before
him at Bury St. Edmunds, at the Spring Assizes in 1664,
as witches. The report was taken in Court during the
trial, but was not published till eighteen years afterwards,
in 1682. Every decade, at that time, saw a progressive
decline in the belief in witchcraft. The person who
published the report was, however, a believer ; and he
considered, he tells us, that ' so exact a relation of this
trial would probably give more satisfaction to a great
many persons, by reason that it is pure matter of fact, and
that evidently demonstrated, than the arguments and
reasons of other very learned men that probably may not
be so intelligible to all readers ; especially, this being
held before a judge whom for his integrity, learning, and
law, hardly any age either before or since could parallel;

[1] Reprinted in *A Collection of Rare and Curious Tracts relating to Witchcraft.* London, 1838.

who not only took a great deal of pains and spent much time in this trial himself, but had the assistance and opinion of several other very eminent and learned persons.' One of these persons was Sir Thomas Browne of Norwich, the author of the *Religio Medici* and of the book on *Vulgar Errors.*

The relation of the trial of Rose Cullender and Amy Duny is indeed most interesting and most instructive, because it shows us so clearly how to live in a certain atmosphere of belief will govern men's conclusions from what they see and hear. To us who do not believe in witches, the evidence on which Rose Cullender and Amy Duny were convicted carries its own natural explanation with it, and itself dispels the charge against them. They were accused of having bewitched a number of children, causing them to have fits, and to bring up pins and nails. Several of the witnesses were poor ignorant people. The weighty evidence in the case was that of Samuel Pacy, a merchant of Lowestoft, two of whose children, Elizabeth and Deborah, of the ages of eleven and nine, were said to have been bewitched. The younger child was too ill to be brought to the Assizes, but the elder was produced in Court. Samuel Pacy, their father, is described as 'a man who carried himself with much soberness during the trial, from whom proceeded no words either of passion or

malice, though his children were so greatly afflicted.'
He deposed that his younger daughter, being lame and
without power in her limbs, had on a sunshiny day in
October ' desired to be carried on the east part of the
house to be set upon the bank which looketh upon the
sea.' While she sat there, Amy Duny, who as well as the
other prisoner is shown by the evidence to have been by
her neighbours commonly reputed a witch, came to the
house to get some herrings. She was refused, and went
away grumbling. At the same moment the child was
seized with violent fits. The doctor who attended her
could not explain them. So ten days afterwards her
father, according to his own deposition, ' by reason of
the circumstances aforesaid, and in regard Amy Duny is
a woman of an ill fame and commonly reported to be a
witch and a sorceress, and for that the said child in her
fits would cry out of Amy Duny as the cause of her
malady, and that she did affright her with apparitions of
her person, as the child in the interval of her fits related,
did suspect the said Amy Duny for a witch, and charged
her with the injury and wrong to his child, and caused
her to be set in the stocks.' While she was there, two
women asked her the reason of the illness of Mr. Pacy's
child. She answered : ' Mr. Pacy keeps a great stir about
his child, but let him stay until he hath done as much by

his children as I have done by mine.' Being asked what she had done to hers, she replied that 'she had been fain to open her child's mouth with a tap to give it victuals.' Two days afterwards Pacy's elder daughter, Elizabeth, was seized with fits like her sister's ; 'insomuch that they could not open her mouth to preserve her life without the help of a tap which they were obliged to use.' The children in their fits would cry out : ' There stands Amy Duny ' or ' Rose Cullender ' (another reputed witch of Lowestoft) ; and, when the fits were over, would relate how they had seen Amy Duny and Rose Cullender shaking their fists at them and threatening them. They said that bees or flies carried into their mouths the pins and nails which they brought up in their fits. During their illness their father sometimes made them read aloud from the New Testament. He 'observed that they would read till they came to the name of *Lord*, or *Jesus*, or *Christ*, and then before they could pronounce either of the said words they would suddenly fall into their fits. But when they came to the name of *Satan* or *Devil* they would clap their fingers upon the book, crying out : " This bites, but makes me speak right well." ' And when their father asked them why they could not pronounce the words *Lord*, or *Jesus*, or *Christ*, they answered : ' Amy Duny saith, I must not use that name.'

It seems almost an impertinence nowadays to suppose, that any one can require telling how self-explanatory
all this is, without recourse to witchcraft and magic.
These poor rickety children, full of disease and with
morbid tricks, have their imagination possessed by the
two famed and dreaded witches of their native place,
of whose prowess they have heard tale after tale, whom
they have often seen with their own eyes, whose presence
has startled one of them in her hour of suffering, and
round whom all those ideas of diabolical agency, in
which they have been nursed, converge and cluster. The
speech of the accused witch in the stocks is the most
natural speech possible, and the fulfilment which her
words received in the course of Elizabeth Pacy's fits is
perfectly natural also. However, Sir Thomas Browne
(who appears in the report of the trial as 'Dr. Brown,
of Norwich, a person of great knowledge'), being desired
to give his opinion on Elizabeth Pacy's case and that
of two other children who on similar evidence were said
to have been bewitched by the accused,—Sir Thomas
Browne

was clearly of opinion that the persons were bewitched ; and
said that in Denmark there had been lately a great discovery
of witches, who used the very same way of afflicting persons
by conveying pins into them, and crooked, as these pins were,

with needles and nails. And his opinion was that the Devil
in such cases did work upon the bodies of men and women
upon a natural foundation, . . . for he conceived that these
swooning fits were natural, and nothing else but what they
call *the mother*, but only heightened to a great excess by the
subtlety of the Devil, co-operating with the malice of these
which we term witches, at whose instance he doth these
villainies.

That was all the light to be got from the celebrated
writer on *Vulgar Errors*. Yet reason, in this trial, was
not left quite without witness :—

At the hearing the evidence, there were divers known
persons, as Mr. Serjeant Keeling, Mr. Serjeant Earl, and
Mr. Serjeant Bernard, present. Mr. Serjeant Keeling
seemed much unsatisfied with it, and thought it not sufficient
to convict the prisoners ; for admitting that the children were
in truth bewitched, yet, said he, it can never be applied to the
prisoners upon the imagination only of the parties afflicted.
For if that might be allowed, no person whatsoever can be
in safety ; for perhaps they might fancy another person, who
might altogether be innocent in such matters.

In order, therefore, the better to establish the guilt
of the prisoners, they were made to touch the children
whom they were said to have bewitched. The children
screamed out at their touch. The children were
'blinded with their own aprons,' and in this condition
were again touched by Rose Cullender ; and again they

screamed out. It was objected, not that the children's
heads were full of Rose Cullender and Amy Duny and of
their infernal dealings with them, but that the children
might be counterfeiting their malady, and pretending to
start at the witch's touch though it had no real power on
them :—

Wherefore, to avoid this scruple, it was privately desired
by the judge, that the Lord Cornwallis, Sir Edward Bacon,
Mr. Serjeant Keeling, and some other gentlemen then in
Court, would attend one of the distempered persons in the
further part of the hall, whilst she was in her fits, and then
to send for one of the witches to try what would then happen,
which they did accordingly. And Amy Duny was conveyed
from the bar and brought to the maid ; they put an apron
before her eyes, and then one other person touched her hand,
which produced the same effect as the touch of the witch did
in the Court. Whereupon the gentlemen returned, openly
protesting that they did believe the whole transaction of this
business was a mere imposture.

This, we are told, 'put the Court and all persons
into a stand. But at length Mr. Pacy did declare that
possibly the maid might be deceived by a suspicion that
the witch touched her when she did not.' And nothing
more likely ; but what does this prove? That the
child's terrors were sincere ; not that the so-called witch
had done the acts alleged against her. However, Mr.
Pacy's solution of the difficulty was readily accepted. If

the children were not shamming out of malice or from a love of imposture, then ' it is very evident that the parties were bewitched, and that when they apprehend that the persons who have done them this wrong are near, or touch them, then, their spirits being more than ordinarily moved with rage and anger, they do use more violent gestures of their bodies.'

Such was the evidence. The accused did not confess themselves guilty. When asked what they had to say for themselves, they replied, as well they might : ' Nothing material to anything that had been proved.' Hale then charged the jury. He did not even go over the evidence to them :—

Only this he acquainted them : that they had two things to inquire after. First, whether or no these children were bewitched ; secondly, whether the prisoners at the bar were guilty of it. That there were such creatures as witches he made no doubt at all. For, first, the Scriptures had affirmed so much ; secondly, the wisdom of all nations had provided laws against such persons, which is an argument of their confidence of such a crime. And such hath been the judgment of this kingdom, as appears by that Act of Parliament which hath provided punishments proportionable to the quality of the offence. And he desired them strictly to observe their evidence, and desired the great God of Heaven to direct their hearts in this weighty thing they had in hand. For to condemn the innocent, and to let the guilty go free, were both an abomination to the Lord.

The jury retired.   In half an hour they came back
with a verdict of *guilty* against both prisoners.   Next
morning the children who had been produced in court
were brought to Hale's lodgings, perfectly restored :—

Mr. Pacy did affirm, that within less than half an hour
after the witches were convicted, they were all of them
restored, and slept well that night ; only Susan Chandler felt
a pain like pricking of pins in her stomach.

And this seems to have removed all shadow of doubt or
misgiving :—

In conclusion, the judge and all the court were fully satisfied
with the verdict, and thereupon gave judgment against the
witches that they should be hanged.   They were much urged
to confess, but would not.   That morning we departed for
Cambridge ; but no reprieve was granted, and they were
executed on Monday, the seventeenth of March (1664) following, but they confessed nothing.

Now, the inference to be drawn from this trial is not
by any means that Hale was 'an imbecile or credulous
enthusiast.'   The whole history of his life and doings dis-
proves it.   But the belief in witchcraft was in the very
atmosphere which Hale breathed, as the belief in miracle
was in the very atmosphere which St. Paul breathed.
What the trial shows us is, that a man of veracity, judgment, and mental power, may have his mind thoroughly
governed, on certain subjects, by a foregone conclusion

as to what is likely and credible. But I will not further
enlarge on the illustration which Hale furnishes to us of
this truth. An illustration of it, with a yet closer appli-
cability to St. Paul, is supplied by another worthy of the
seventeenth century.

### 3.

The worthy in question is very little known, and I
rejoice to have an opportunity of mentioning him. *John
Smith!*—the name does not sound promising. He died
at the age of thirty-four, having risen to no higher post
in the world than a college-fellowship. 'He proceeded
leisurely by orderly steps,' says Simon Patrick, afterwards
Bishop of Ely, who preached his funeral-sermon, 'not to
what he could get, but to what he was fit to undertake.'
John Smith, born in 1618 near Oundle in Northampton-
shire, was admitted a scholar of Emanuel College at
Cambridge in 1636, a fellow of Queen's College in 1644.
He became a tutor and preacher in his college ; died
there, 'after a tedious sickness,' on the 7th of August,
1652, and was buried in the college-chapel. He was one
of that band of Cambridge Platonists, or *latitude men*, as
in their own day they were called, whom Burnet has well
described as those ' who, at Cambridge, studied to propagate better thoughts, to take men off from being in

parties, or from narrow notions, from superstitious con-
ceits and fierceness about opinions.' Principal Tulloch
has done an excellent work in seeking to reawaken our
interest in this noble but neglected group. His book[1]
is delightful, and it has, at the same time, the most
serious value. But in his account of his worthies, Principal Tulloch has given, I cannot but think, somewhat
too much space to their Platonic philosophy, to their
disquisitions on spirit and incorporeal essence. It is not
by these that they merited to live, or that, having passed
away from men's minds, they will be brought back to
them. It is by their extraordinary simple, profound, and
just conception of religion. Placed between the sacer-
dotal religion of the Laudian clergy on the one side, and
the notional religion of the Puritans on the other, they
saw the sterility, the certain doom, of both;—saw that
stand permanently such developments of religion could
not, inasmuch as Christianity was not what either of
them supposed, but was a *temper*, a *behaviour*.

Their immediate recompense was a religious isolation
of two centuries. The religious world was not then ripe
for more than the High Church conception of Christianity
on the one hand, or the Puritan conception on the other.

---

[1] *Rational Theology and Christian Philosophy in England in the
Seventeenth Century*; 2nd edition, Edinburgh and London, 1874.

The Cambridge band ceased to acquire recruits, and dis-
appeared with the century. Individuals knew and used
their writings ; Bishop Wilson of Sodor and Man, in
particular, had profited by them. But they made no
broad and clear mark. And this was in part for the
reason already assigned, in part because what passed for
their great work was that revival of a spiritualist and Platonic philosophy, to which Principal Tulloch, as I have
said, seems to me to have given too much prominence.
By this attempted revival they could not and cannot
live. The theology and writings of Owen are not more
extinct than the *Intellectual System* of Cudworth. But
in a history of the Cambridge Platonists, works of the
magnitude of Cudworth's *Intellectual System of the Universe* must necessarily, perhaps, fill a large space. Therefore it is not so much a history of this group which is
wanted, as a republication of such of their utterances as
show us their real spirit and power. Their spiritual
brother, 'the ever memorable Mr. John Hales,' must
certainly, notwithstanding that he was at Oxford, not
Cambridge, be classed along with them. The remains of
Hales of Eton, the sermons and aphorisms of Whichcote,
the sermon preached by Cudworth before the House of
Commons with the second sermon printed as a com-
panion to it, single sayings and maxims of Henry More,

and the *Select Discourses* of John Smith,—there are our
documents! In them lies enshrined what the *latitude
men* have of value for us.   It were well if Principal
Tulloch would lay us under fresh obligations by himself
extracting this and giving it to us ; but given some day,
and by some hand, it will surely be.

For Hales and the Cambridge Platonists here offer,
formulated with sufficient distinctness, a conception of
religion, true, long obscured, and for which the hour of
light has at last come.   Their productions will not, indeed, take rank as great works of literature and style.
It is not to the history of literature that Whichcote and
Smith belong, but to the history of religion.   Their contemporaries were Bossuet, Pascal, Taylor, Barrow.   It is
in the history of literature that these men are mainly
eminent, although they may also be classed, of course,
among religious writers.   What counts highest in the
history of religion as such, is, however, to give what at
critical moments the religious life of mankind needs and
can use.   And it will be found that the Cambridge
Platonists, although neither epoch-making philosophers
nor epoch-making men of letters, have in their conception of religion a boon for the religious wants of our own
time, such as we shall demand in vain from the soul and
poetry of Taylor, from the sense and vigour of Barrow,

from the superb exercitations of Bossuet, or the passion-filled reasoning and rhetoric of Pascal.

The *Select Discourses* of John Smith, collected and published from his papers after his death, are, in my opinion, by much the most considerable work left to us by this Cambridge school. They have a right to a place in English literary history. Yet the main value of the *Select Discourses* is, I repeat, religious, not literary. Their grand merit is that they insist on the profound *natural truth* of Christianity, and thus base it upon a ground which will not crumble under our feet. Signal and rare indeed is the merit, in a theological instructor, of presenting Christianity to us in this fashion. Christianity is true ; but in general the whole plan for grounding and buttressing it chosen by our theological instructors is false, and, since it is false, it must fail us sooner or later. I have often thought that if candidates for orders were simply, in preparing for their examination, to read and digest Smith's great discourse, *On the Excellency and Nobleness of True Religion*, together with M. Reuss's *History of Christian Theology at the time of the Apostles*, and nothing further except the Bible itself, we might have, perhaps, a hope of at last getting, as our national guides in religion, a clergy which could tell its bearings and steer its way, instead of being, as we now see it, too often conspicuously at a loss to do either.

Singularly enough, about fifteen years before the trial at Bury St. Edmunds of the Lowestoft witches, John Smith, the author of the *Select Discourses*, had in those very eastern counties to deliver his mind on the matter of witchcraft. On Lady-day every year, a Fellow of Queen's College, Cambridge, was required to preach at Huntingdon a sermon against witchcraft and diabolical contracts. Smith, as one of the Fellows of Queen's, had to preach this sermon. It is printed tenth and last of his *Select Discourses*, with the title : *A Christian's Conflicts and Conquests; or, a Discourse concerning the Devil's Active Enmity and Continual Hostility against Man, the Warfare of a Christian Life, the Certainty of Success and Victory in this Spiritual Warfare, the Evil and Horridness of Magical Arts and Rites, Diabolical Contracts, &c.* The discourse has for its text the words : ' Resist the devil, and he will flee from you.'

The preacher sets out with the traditional account of 'the prince of darkness, who, having once stained the original beauty and glory of the divine workmanship, is continually striving to mould and shape it more and more into his own likeness.' He says :—

It were perhaps a vain curiosity to inquire whether the number of evil spirits exceeds the number of men ; but this is too, too certain, that we never want the secret and latent

attendance of them. . . . Those evil spirits are not yet cast
out of the world into outer darkness, though it be prepared
for them ; the bottomless pit hath not yet shut its mouth upon
them.

And he concludes his sermon with a reflexion and a
caution, called for, he says, by the particular occasion.
The reflexion is that—

Did we not live in a world of professed wickedness, wherein
so many men's sins go in open view before them to judgment,
it might be thought needless to persuade men to resist the
devil when he appears in his own colours to make merchan-
dise of them, and comes in a formal way to bargain with
them for their souls ; that which human nature, however
enthralled to sin and Satan in a more mysterious way, abhors,
and none admit but those who are quite degenerated from
human kind.

And he adds the caution, that—

The use of any arts, rites, or ceremonies not understood,
of which we can give no rational or divine account, this
indeed is nothing else but a kind of magic which the devil
himself owns and gives life to, though he may not be corpo-
really present, or require presently any further covenant from
the users of them. The devil, no question, is present to all
his own rites and ceremonies, though men discern him not,
and may upon the use of them secretly produce those effects
which may gain credit to them. Among these rites we may
reckon insignificant forms of words, with their several modes
and manner of pronunciation, astrological arts, and whatsoever else pretends to any strange effects which we cannot

with good reason either ascribe to God or nature. As God
will only be conversed withal in a way of light and understanding, so the devil loves to be conversed with in a way of
darkness and obscurity.

But between his exordium and his conclusion the real
man appears. Like Hale, Smith seems to have accepted
the belief in witchcraft and in diabolical contracts which
was regnant in his day. But when he came to deal with
the belief as an idea influencing thought and conduct, he
could not take it as the people around him took it. It
was his nature to seek a firm ground for the ideas
admitted by him; above all, when these ideas had
bearings upon religion. And for witchcraft and diabolical
operation, in the common conception of them as external
things, he could find no solid ground, for there was none;
and therefore he could not so use them. See, therefore,
how profoundly they are transformed by him! After his
exordium he makes an entirely fresh departure :—' When
we say the devil is continually busy with us, I mean not
only some apostate spirit as one particular being, but
that spirit of apostasy which is lodged in all men's
natures.' Here, in this *spirit of apostasy which is lodged
in all men's natures*, Smith had what was at bottom
experimental and real. And the whole effort of the
sermon is to substitute this for what men call the devil,

hell, fiends, and witches, as an object for their serious
thought and strenuous resistance :—

As the kingdom of heaven is not so much without men
as within, as our Saviour tells us ; so the tyranny of the devil
and hell is not so much in some external things as in the
qualities and dispositions of men's minds.   And as the enjoying of God, and conversing with him, consists not so much
in a change of place as in the participation of the divine
nature and in our assimilation unto God ; so our conversing
with the devil is not so much by a mutual local presence as
by an imitation of a wicked and sinful nature derived upon
men's own souls. . . . He that allows himself in any sin, or
useth an unnatural dalliance with any vice, does nothing else
in reality than entertain an *incubus demon.*

This, however, was by no means a view of diabolical
possession acceptable to the religious world and to its
Puritan ministers :—

I know these expressions will seem to some very harsh
and unwelcome ; but I would beseech them to consider what
they will call that spirit of malice and envy, that spirit of
pride, ambition, vain-glory, covetousness, injustice, unclean-
ness, &c., that commonly reigns so much and acts so violently
in the minds and lives of men.   Let us speak the truth, and
call things by their own names ; so much as there is of sin in
any man, so much there is of the diabolical nature.   Why do
we defy the devil so much with our tongues, while we entertain him in our hearts ?   As men's love to God is ordinarily
nothing else but the mere tendency of their natures to something that hath the name of God put upon it, without any

clear or distinct apprehensions of him, so their hatred of the devil is commonly nothing else but an inward displacency of nature against something entitled by the devil's name. And as they commonly make a God like to themselves, such a one as they can but comply with and love, so they make a devil most unlike to themselves, which may be anything but what they themselves are, that so they may most freely spend their anger and hatred upon him ; just as they say of some of the Ethiopians, who used to paint the devil white because they themselves are black. This is a strange, merry kind of maddess, whereby men sportingly bereave themselves of the supremest good, and insure themselves, as much as may be, to hell and misery ; they may thus cheat themselves for a while, but the eternal foundation of the Divine Being is immutable and unchangeable. And where we find wisdom, justice, loveliness, goodness, love, and glory in their highest elevations and most unbounded dimensions, that is He ; and where we find any true participations of these, there is a true communication of God ; and a defection from these is the essence of sin and the foundation of hell.

Finally (and I quote the more freely because the author whom I quote is so little known),—finally our preacher goes on to even confute his own exordium :—

It was the fond error of the Manichees that there was some solid *principium mali,* which, having an eternal existence of its own, had also a mighty and uncontrollable power from within itself whereby it could forcibly enter into the souls of men, and, seating itself there, by some hidden influences irresistibly incline and inforce them to evil. But we ourselves uphold that kingdom of darkness, which else would tumble down and slide into that nothing from whence it

came.  *All sin and vice is our own creature;* we only give
life to them which indeed are our death, and would soon
wither and fade away did we substract our concurrence from
them.

O fortunate Huntingdon Church, which admitted for
even one day such a counterblast to the doctrines then
sounding from every pulpit, and still enjoined by Sir
Robert Phillimore !

That a man shares an error of the minds around him
and of the times in which he lives, proves nothing
against his being a man of veracity, judgment, and
mental power.  This we saw by the case of Hale.  But
here, in our Cambridge Platonist, we have a man who
accepts the erroneous belief in witchcraft, professes it
publicly, preaches on it ; and yet is not only a man of
veracity and intelligence, but actually manages to give
to the error adopted by him a turn, an aspect, which
indicates its erroneousness.  Not only is he of help to
us generally, in spite of his error ; he is of help to us in
respect of that very error itself.

Now, herein is really a most striking analogy between
our little-known divine of the seventeenth century and
the great Apostle of the Gentiles.  St. Paul's writings
are in every one's hands.  I have myself discussed his
doctrine at length.  And for our present purpose there is

no need of elaborate exposition and quotation. Every one knows how St. Paul declares his belief that ' Christ rose again the third day, and was seen of Cephas, then of the twelve ; after that, he was seen of above five hundred brethren at once.'[1] Those who do not admit the miraculous can yet well conceive how such a belief arose, and was entertained by St. Paul. *The resurrection of the just* was at that time a ruling idea of a Jew's mind. Herod at once, and without difficulty, supposed that John the Baptist was *risen from the dead.* The Jewish people without difficulty supposed that Jesus might be one of the old prophets, *risen from the dead.* In telling the story of the crucifixion men added, quite naturally, that when it was consummated, ' many bodies of the saints which slept *arose and appeared unto many.*' Jesus himself, moreover, had in his lifetime spoken frequently of his own coming resurrection. Such beliefs as the belief in bodily resurrection were thus a part of the mental atmosphere in which the first Christians lived. It was inevitable that they should believe their Master to have risen again in the body, and that St. Paul, in becoming a Christian, should receive the belief and build upon it.

But Paul, like our Cambridge Platonist, instinctively sought in an idea, used for religion, a side by which

[1] I *Cor.*, xv, 4, 5, 6.

the idea could enter into his religious experience and become real to him. No such side could be afforded by the mere external fact and miracle of Christ's bodily resurrection. Paul, therefore, as is well known, by a prodigy of religious insight seized another aspect for the resurrection than the aspect of physical miracle. He presented resurrection as a spiritual rising which could be appropriated and enacted in our own living experience. 'If One died in the name of all, then all died ; and he died in the name of all, that they who live should no more live unto themselves, but unto him who died and rose again in their name.'[1] Dying became thus no longer a bodily dying, but a dying to sin ; rising to life no longer a bodily resurrection, but a living to God. St. Paul here comes, therefore, upon that very idea of death and resurrection which was the central idea of Jesus himself. At the very same moment that he shares and professes the popular belief in Christ's miraculous bodily resurrection,—the idea by which our Saviour's own idea of resurrection has been overlaid and effaced,—St. Paul seizes also this other truer idea or is seized by it, and bears unconscious witness to its unique legitimacy.

Where, then, is the force of that *argument of despair,* as we called it, that if St. Paul vouches for the bodily re-

[1] II *Cor.*, v, 14, 15.

surrection of Jesus and for his appearance after it, and is
mistaken in so vouching, then he must be 'an imbecile
and credulous enthusiast,' untruthful, unprofitable? We
see that for a man to believe in preternatural incidents,
of a kind admitted by the common belief of his time,
proves nothing at all against his general truthfulness and
sagacity. Nay, we see that even while affirming such
preternatural incidents, he may with profound insight
seize the true and natural aspect of them, the aspect
which will survive and profit when the miraculous aspect
has faded. He may give us, in the very same work,
current error and also fruitful and profound new truth,
the error's future corrective.


4.


But I am treating of these matters for the last time.
And those who no longer admit, in religion, the old
basis of the preternatural, I see them encountered by
scruples of their own, as well as by scruples raised by
their opponents. Their opponents, the partisans of miracle, require them if they refuse to admit miracle to
throw aside as imbecile or untruthful all their instructors
and inspirers who have ever admitted it. But they themselves, too, are sometimes afraid, not only of being called
inconsistent and insincere, but of really meriting to be

called so, if they do not break decidedly with the religion
in which they have been brought up, if they at all try still
to conform to it and to use it.   I have now before me
a remarkable letter, in which the writer says :—

There is nothing I and many others should like better
than to take service as ministers in the Church as *a national
society for the promotion of goodness* ; but how can we do so,
when we have first to declare our belief in a quantity of
things which every intelligent man rejects ?

Now, as I have examined the question whether a man
who rejects miracles must break with St. Paul because
Paul asserted them, so let me, before I end, examine the
question whether such a man must break with the
Church of his country and childhood.

Certainly it is a strong thing to suppose, as the writer
of the above-quoted letter supposes, a man taking orders
in the Church of England who accepts, say, the view of
Christianity offered in *Literature and Dogma*.   For the
Church of England presents as science, and as necessary to salvation, what it is the very object of that book
to show to be *not* science and *not* necessary to salvation.
And  at his ordination a man is required to declare that
he, too, accepts this for science, as the Church does.   Formerly a deacon subscribed to the Thirty-nine Articles,
and to a declaration that he acknowledged ‘ all and every

the articles therein contained to be agreeable to the word
of God.' A clerk, admitted to a benefice with cure,
declared 'his unfeigned assent and consent to all the
matters contained in the Articles.' At present, I think,
all that is required is a general consent to whatever is
contained in the Book of Common Prayer. But the
Book of Common Prayer contains the Thirty-nine
Articles. And the Eighth Article declares the Three
Creeds to be science, science 'thoroughly to be received
and believed.' Now, whether one professes 'an unfeigned assent and consent' to this Article, as contained
among the Thirty-nine Articles, or merely 'a general
consent' to it, as contained in the Prayer Book, one
certainly, by consenting to it at all, professes to receive
the Three Creeds as science, and as true science. And
this is the very point where it is important to be explicit
and firm. Whatever else the Three Creeds may be,
they are not science, truly formulating the Christian religion. And no one who feels convinced that they are
not, can sincerely say that he gives even a general consent to whatever is contained in the Prayer Book, or can
at present, therefore, be ordained a minister of the
Church of England.

The obstacle, it will be observed, is in a test which
lies outside of the Ordination Service itself. The test is

a remnant of the system of subscriptions and tests
formerly employed so vigorously. It was meant as a
reduction and alleviation of that old yoke. To obtain
such a reduction seemed once to generous and ardent
minds, and indeed once was, a very considerable conquest. But the times move rapidly, and even the re-
duced test has now a great power of exclusion. If it
were possible for Liberal politicians ever to deal seriously with religion, they would turn their minds to the
removal of a test of this sort, instead of playing with
political dissent or marriage with a deceased wife's sister.
The Ordination Service itself, on a man's entrance into
orders, and the use of the Church services afterwards,
are a sufficient engagement. Things were put into the
Ordination Service which one might have wished otherwise. Some of them are gone. The introduction of the
Oath of Supremacy was a part, no doubt, of all that *lion
and unicorn* business which is too plentiful in our Prayer
Book, on which Dr. Newman has showered such ex-
quisite raillery, and of which only the Philistine element
in our race prevents our seeing the ridiculousness. But
the Oath of Supremacy has now no longer a place in the
Ordination Service. Apart, however, from such mere
matters of taste, there was and still is the requirement, in
the Ordering of Deacons, of a declaration of unfeigned

belief in all the canonical Scriptures of the Old and New Testament. Perhaps this declaration can have a construction put upon it which makes it admissible. But by its form of expression it recalls, and appears to adopt, the narrow and letter-bound views of Biblical inspiration formerly prevalent,—prevalent with the Fathers as well as with the Reformers,—but which are now, I suppose, generally abandoned. I imagine the clergy themselves would be glad to substitute for this declaration the words in the Ordering of Priests, where the candidate declares himself ' persuaded that the Holy Scriptures contain sufficiently all doctrine required for eternal salvation through faith in Jesus Christ.' These words present no difficulty, nor is there any other serious difficulty, that I can see, raised by the Ordination Service for either priests or deacons. The declaration of a general consent to the Articles is another matter ; although perhaps, in the present temper of men's minds, it could not easily be got rid of.

The last of Butler's jottings in his memorandum-book is a prayer to be delivered ' from *offendiculum* of scrupulousness.' He was quite right. Religion is a matter where scrupulousness has been far too active, producing most serious mischief ; and where it is singularly out of place. I am the very last person to wish to deny it. Those, therefore, who declared their consent to the

Articles long ago, and who are usefully engaged in the ministry of the Church, would in my opinion do exceedingly ill to disquiet themselves about having given a consent to the Articles formerly, when things had not moved to the point where they are now, and did not appear to men's minds as they now appear. ' Forgetting those things which are behind and reaching forth to those things which are before,' should in these cases be a man's motto. The Church is properly a national society for the promotion of goodness. For him it is such ; he ministers in it as such. He has never to use the Articles, never to rehearse them. He has to rehearse the prayers and services of the Church. Much of these he may rehearse as the literal, beautiful rendering of what he himself feels and believes. The rest he may rehearse as an approximative rendering of it ;—as language *thrown out* by other men, in other times, at immense objects which deeply engaged their affections and awe, and which deeply engage his also ; objects concerning which, moreover, adequate statement is impossible. To him, therefore, this approximative part of the prayers and services which he rehearses will be poetry. It is a great error to think that whatever is thus perceived to be poetry ceases to be available in religion. The noblest races are those which know how to make the most serious use of poetry.

But the Articles are plain prose. They aim at the exactitude of a legal document. They are a precise profession of belief, formulated by men of our own nation three hundred years ago, in regard, amongst other things, to parts of those services of the Church of which we have been speaking. At all points the Articles are, and must be, inadequate; but into the question of their general inadequacy we need not now enter. One point is sufficient. They present the Creeds as science, exact science; and this, at the present time of day, very many a man cannot accept. He cannot rightly, then, profess in any way to accept it; cannot, in consequence, take orders.

But it is easy for such a man to exaggerate to himself the barrier between himself and popular religion. The barrier is not so great as he may suppose; and it is expedient for him rather to think it less great than it is, than more great. It will insensibly dwindle, the more that he, and other serious men who think as he does, strive so far as they can to act as if it did not exist. It will stand stiff and bristling the more they act as if it were insurmountable. The Church of our country is to be considered as a national Christian society for the promotion of goodness, to which a man cannot but wish well, and in which he might rejoice to minister. To a right-judging mind, the cardinal points of belief for either the member or the

minister of such a society are but two : *Salvation by Righteousness* and *Righteousness by Jesus Christ.* Salvation by
Righteousness,—there is the sum of the Old Testament :
Righteousness by Jesus Christ,—there is the sum of the
New. For popular religion, the cardinal points of belief
are of course a good deal more numerous. Not without
adding many others could popular religion manage to
benefit by the first-named two. But the first-named two
have its adherence. It is from the very effort to benefit
by them that it has added all the rest. The services of the
Church are full of direct recognitions of the two really
essential points of Christian belief : *Salvation by Righteousness* and *Righteousness by Jesus Christ.* They are full,
too, of what may be called approximate recognitions of
them ;—efforts of the human mind, in its gradual growth,
to develop them, to fix them, to buttress them, to make
them clearer to itself, to bring them nearer, by the addition
of miracle and metaphysic. This is poetry. The Articles
say that this poetry is exact prose. But the Articles are
no more a real element of the Prayer Book than Brady
and Tate's metrical version of the Psalms, which has
now happily been expelled. And even while the Articles
continue to stand in the Prayer Book, yet a layman can
use the Prayer Book as if they and their definitions did
not exist. To be ordained, however, one must adhere to
their definitions. But, putting the Articles aside, will a

layman, since he is free, would a clergyman, if he were free, desire to abandon the use of all those parts of the Prayer Book which are to be regarded as merely approximative recognitions of its two central truths, and as poetry? Must all such parts one day, as our experience widens and this view of their character comes to prevail, be eliminated from our public worship? The question is a most important one.

For although the Comtists, by the mouth of their most eloquent spokesman, tell us that ' 'tis the pedantry of sect alone which can dare to monopolise to a special creed those precious heirlooms of a common race,' the ideas and power of religion, and propose to remake religion for us with new and improved personages, and rites, and words; yet it is certain that here as elsewhere the wonderful force of habit tells, and that the power of religious ideas over us does not spring up at call, but is intimately dependent upon particular names and practices and forms of expression which have gone along with it ever since we can remember, and which have created special sentiments in us. I believe, indeed, that the eloquent spokesman of the Comtists errs at the very outset. I believe that the power of religion does of nature belong, in a unique way, to the Bible and to Christianity, and that it is no pedantry of sect which affirms this, but experience. Yet even were it as he supposes, and

Christianity were not the one proper bringer-in of righteousness and of the reign of the Spirit and of eternal life, and these were to be got as well elsewhere, but still we ourselves had learnt all we know about them from Christianity,—then for us to be taught them in some other guise, by some other instructor, would be almost impossible. Habits and associations are not formed in a day. Even if the very young have time enough before them to learn to associate religion with new personages and precepts, the middle-aged and the old have not, and must shrink from such an endeavour. *Mane nobiscum, Domine, nam advesperascit.*

Nay, but so prodigious a revolution does the changing the whole form and feature of religion turn out to be, that it even unsettles all other things too, and brings back chaos. When it happens, the civilisation and the society to which it happens are disintegrated, and men have to begin again. This is what took place when Christianity superseded the old religion of the Pagan world. People may say that there is a fund of ideas common to all religions, at least to all religions of superior and civilised races; and that the personages and precepts, the form and feature, of one such religion may be exchanged for those of another, or for those of some new religion devised by an enlightened eclecticism, and the world

may go on all the while without much disturbance.
There were philosophers who thought so when Paganism
was going out and Christianity coming in. But they were
mistaken. The whole civilisation of the Roman world
was disintegrated by the change, and men had, I say, to
begin again. So immense is the sentiment created by
the things to which we have been used in religion, so
profound is the wrench at parting with them, so incalculable is the trouble and distraction caused by it.
Now, we can hardly conceive modern civilisation
breaking up as the Roman did, and men beginning
again as they did in the fifth century. But the improbability of this implies the improbability, too, of our seeing
all the form and feature of Christianity disappear,—of
the religion of Christendom. For so vast a revolution
would this be, that it would involve the other.

These considerations are of force, I think, in regard
to all radical change in the language of the Prayer Book.
It has created sentiments deeper than we can see or
measure. Our feeling does not connect itself with *any*
language about righteousness and religion, but with *that*
language. Very much of it we can all use in its literal
acceptation. But the question is as to those parts
which we cannot. Of course, those who can take them
literally will still continue to use them. But for us also,

who can no longer put the literal meaning on them which others do, and which we ourselves once did, they retain a power, and something in us vibrates to them. And not unjustly. For these old forms of expression were men's sincere attempt to set forth with due honour what we honour also ; and the sense of the attempt gives a beauty and an emotion to the words, and makes them poetry. The Creeds are in this way an attempt to exalt to the utmost, by assigning to him all the characters which to mankind seemed to confer exaltation, Jesus Christ. I have elsewhere called the Apostles' Creed the popular science of Christianity, and the Nicene Creed its learned science ; and in one view of them they are so. But in another and a better view of them, they are, the one its popular poetry, the other its learned or,—to borrow the word which Schopenhauer applied to Hegel's philosophy,—its *scholastic poetry*. The one Creed exalts Jesus by concrete images, the other by an imaginative play of abstract ideas. These two Creeds are the august am- plifications, or the high elucidations, which came naturally to the human spirit working in love and awe upon that inexhaustible theme of profound truth : *Salvation through Jesus Christ*. As such, they are poetry for us ; and poetry consecrated, moreover, by having been on the tongue of all our forefathers for two thousand years, and

on our own tongue ever since we were born. As such,
then, we can *feel* them, even when we no longer take
them literally ; while, as approximations to a profound
truth, we can *use* them. We cannot call them science,
as the Articles would have us; but we can still feel them
and still use them. And if we can do this with the
Creeds, still more can we do it with the rest of the services
in the Prayer Book.

As to the very and true foundations, therefore, of the
Christian religion,—the belief that salvation is by righteousness, and that righteousness is by Jesus Christ,—we
are, in fact, at one with the religious world in general. As
to the true object of the Church, that it is the promotion
of goodness, we are at one with them also. And as to
the form and wording of religion,—a form and wording
consecrated by so many years and memories,—even as to
this we need not break with them either. They and we
can remain in sympathy. Some changes will no doubt
befall the Prayer Book as time goes on. Certain things
will drop away from its services, other things will replace
them. But such change will happen, not in a sweeping
way ;—it will come very gradually, and by the general
wish. It will be brought about, not by a spirit of scrupulosity, innovation, and negation, but by a prevalent
impulse to express in our church-services somewhat which

is felt to need expression, and to be not sufficiently expressed there already.

After all, the great confirmation to a man in believing
that the cardinal points of our religion are far fewer and
simpler than is commonly supposed, is that such was
surely the belief of Jesus himself. And in like manner,
the great reason for continuing to use the familiar language
of the religion around us as approximative language, and
as poetry, although we cannot take it literally, is that
such was also the practice of Jesus. For evidently it was
so. And evidently, again, the immense misapprehension
of Jesus and of his meaning, by popular religion, comes
in part from such having been his practice. But if Jesus
used this way of speaking in spite of its plainly leading
to such misapprehension, it must have been because it
was the best way and the only one. For it was not by introducing a brand-new religious language, and by parting
with all the old and cherished images, that popular religion could be transformed; but by keeping the old
language and images, and as far as possible conveying
into them the soul of the new Christian ideal.

When Jesus talked of the Son of Man coming in his
glory with the holy angels, setting the good on his right
hand and the bad on his left, and sending away the bad
into everlasting fire prepared for the devil and his angels,

was he speaking literally? Did Jesus mean that all this
would actually happen ? Popular religion supposes so.
Yet very many religious people, even now, suppose that
Jesus was but using the figures of Messianic judgment
familiar to his hearers, in order to impress upon them
his main point :—what sort of spirit and of practice did
really tend to salvation, and what did not. And surely
almost every one must perceive, that when Jesus spoke
to his disciples of their sitting on thrones judging the
twelve tribes of Israel, or of their drinking new wine
with him in the kingdom of God, he was adopting their
material images and beliefs, and was not speaking literally. Yet their Master's thus adopting their material
images and beliefs could not but confirm the disciples in
them. And so it did, and Christendom, too, after them ;
yet in this way, apparently, Jesus chose to proceed. But
some one may say, that Jesus used this language because
he himself shared the materialistic notions of his disciples
about the kingdom of God, and thought that coming upon
the clouds, and sitting upon thrones, and drinking wine,
would really occur in it, and was mistaken in thinking
so. And yet there are plain signs that this cannot be
the right account of the matter, and that Jesus did not
really share the beliefs of his disciples or conceive the
kingdom of God as they did. For they manifestly

thought,—even the wisest of them, and after their Master's
death as well as before it,—that this kingdom was to be
a sudden, miraculous, outward transformation of things,
which was to come about very soon and in their own lifetime.   Nevertheless they themselves report Jesus saying
what is in direct contradiction to all this.   They report
him describing the kingdom of God as an inward change
requiring to be spread over an immense time, and
coming about by natural means and gradual growth, not
suddenly, miraculously.   Jesus compares the kingdom of
God to a grain of mustard seed and to a handful of leaven.
He says : 'So is the kingdom of God, as a man may cast
seed in the ground, and may go to bed and get up night
and day, and the seed shoots and extends he knoweth
not how.'[1]   Jesus told his disciples, moreover, that the
good news of the kingdom had to be preached *to the whole
world.*   The whole world must first be evangelised, no
work of one generation, but of centuries and centuries ;
and then, but not till then, should *the end*, the last day,
the new world, the grand transformation of which Jewish
heads were so full, finally come.   True, the disciples also
make Jesus speak as if he fancied this end to be as near
as they did.   But it is quite manifest that Jesus spoke to
them, at different times, of two *ends* : one, the end of the

---

[1] Mark, iv, 26, 27.

Jewish state and nation, which any one who could ' discern
the signs of that time ' might foresee ; the other, the end
of the world, the instatement of God's kingdom ;—and
that they confused the two ends together.   Undeniably,
therefore, Jesus saw things in a way very different from
theirs, and much truer.   And if he uses their materialising
language and imagery, then, it cannot have been because
he shared their illusions.   Nevertheless, he uses it.

And the more we examine the whole language of the
Gospels, the more we shall find it to be not language all
of the speaker's own, and invented by him for the first
time, but to be full of reminiscence and quotation.   How
deeply all the speakers' minds are governed by the
contents of one or two chapters in Daniel, everybody
knows.   It is impossible to understand anything of the
New Testament, without bearing in mind that the main
pivot, on which all that is said turns, is supplied by half
a dozen verses of Daniel.   ' The God of heaven shall set
up a kingdom which shall never be destroyed, and shall
stand for ever.   There shall be a time of trouble, such as
never was since there was a nation even to that time.   I
beheld, till the thrones were cast down, and the Ancient
of days did sit ; and, behold, one like the Son of man
came with the clouds of heaven, and came to the Ancient
of days ; the judgment was set and the books were

opened. And many of them that sleep in the dust of the earth shall awake, some to everlasting life, and some to shame and everlasting contempt.'[1] The language of this group of texts, I say, governs the whole language of the New Testament speakers. The disciples use it literally, Jesus uses it as poetry. But all use it.

Those texts from Daniel almost every reader of the Bible knows. But unless a man has an exceedingly close acquaintance with the prophets, he can have no notion, I think, how very much in the speeches of Jesus is not original language of his own, but is language of the Old Testament,—the religious language on which both he and his hearers had been nourished,—adopted by Jesus, and with a sense of his own communicated to it. There is hardly a trait in the great apocalyptic speech of the twenty-fourth chapter of St. Matthew, which has not its original in some prophet. Even where the scope of Jesus is most profoundly new and his own, his phrase is still, as far as may be, old. In the institution of the Lord's Supper his *new covenant* is a phrase from the admirable and forward-pointing prophecy in the thirty-first chapter of Jeremiah.[2] The *covenant in my blood* points to Exodus,[3] and probably, also, to an expression in that strange but then popular

[1] Dan., ii, 44 ; xii, 1, 2 ; vii, 9, 10, 13.
[2] Verses 31-34.                    [3] *Ex.*, xxiv, 8.

medley, the book of Zechariah.[1]  These phrases, familiar
to himself and to his hearers, Jesus willingly adopted.

But if we confine to the Old Testament alone our
search for parallel passages, we shall have a quite insufficient notion of the extent to which the language of Jesus
is not his own original language, but language and
images adopted from what was current at the time.  It is
this which gives such pre-eminent value to the Book of
Enoch.  That book,—quoted, as every one will remember, in the Epistle of Jude,[2]—explains what would certainly appear, if we had not this explanation, to be an
enlargement and heightening by Jesus, in speaking about
the end of the world, of the materialistic data furnished by
the Old Testament.  For if he thus added to them, it may
be said, he must surely have taken them literally.  But
the Book of Enoch exhibits just the farther stage reached
by these data, between the earlier decades of the second
century before Christ when the Book of Daniel was
written, and the later decades to which belongs the Book
of Enoch.  And just this farther growth of Messianic
language and imagery it was, with which the minds of the
contemporaries of Jesus were familiar.  And in speaking
to them Jesus had to deal with this familiarity.  Unca-
nonical, therefore, though the Book of Enoch be,—for it

came too late, and perhaps contains things too strange, for
admission into the Canon,—it is full of interest, and every
one should read it. The Hebrew original and the Greek
version, as is well known, are lost ; but the book passed
into the Æthiopic Bible, and an Æthiopic manuscript of
it was brought to this country from Abyssinia by Bruce,
the traveller. The first translator and editor of it, Archbishop Laurence, did his work, Orientalists say, imperfectly, and the English version cannot be trusted. There
is an excellent German version ; but I wish that the Bishop
of Gloucester and Bristol, who is, I believe, an Æthiopic
scholar, would give us the book correctly in English.

The Book of Enoch has the names and terms which
are already familiar to us from the Old Testament : Head
or Ancient of days, Son of man, Son of God, Messiah.
It has in frequent use a designation for God, *the Lord of
Spirits*, and designations for the Messiah, *the Chosen One,
the Just One*, which we come upon in the New Testament,[1] but which the New Testament did not, apparently,
get from the Old. It has the angels accompanying the Son
of Man to judgment, and the Son of Man 'sitting on the
throne of his glory.' It has, again and again, the well-
known phrase of the New Testament : *the day of judg-*

---

[1] *The Father of Spirits* in *Hebrews*, xii, 9 ; *the Chosen One* in
*Luke*, xxii, 35 , *the Just One* in *Acts*, xxii, 14.

*ment*; it has its outer darkness and its hell-fire. It has
its beautiful expression, *children of light.* These additions to the Old Testament language had passed, when
Jesus Christ came, into the religion of the time. He did
not create them, but he found them and used them. He
employed, as sanctions of his doctrine, his contemporaries' ready-made notions of hell and judgment, just as
Socrates did. He talked of the outer darkness and the
unquenchable fire, as Socrates talked of the rivers of
Tartarus. And often, when Jesus used phrases which
now seem to us to be his own, he was adopting phrases
made current by the Book of Enoch. When he said :
' It were better for that man he had never been born ; '
when he said : ' Rejoice because your names are written
in heaven ; ' when he said : ' Their angels do always
behold the face of my Father which is in heaven ; ' when
he said : ' The brother shall deliver up the brother to
death and the father the child ; ' when he said : ' Then
shall the righteous shine forth as the sun in the kingdom
of their Father,' he was remembering the book of Enoch.
When he said : ' Tell it to *the church* ; ' when he said to
Peter : ' Thou art Peter, and upon this rock will I build
*my church*, and the gates of hell shall not prevail against
it,'—expressions which, because of the word *church*, some
reject, and others make the foundation for the most illu-

sory pretensions,—Jesus was but recalling the Book of
Enoch.   For in that book the expression, *the company* or
*congregation* (in Greek *ecclesia*) *of the just* or *righteous*,—of
the destined rulers of the coming kingdom of the saints,
—has become a consecrated phrase.   The Messiah, the
founder of that kingdom, is the Just One ; ' the congregation of the just ' are those who follow the Just One, the
Just One's company or *ecclesia*.   When Peter, therefore,
made his ardent declaration of faith, Jesus answered :
' Rock is thy name, and on this rock will I build my company, and the power of death shall not prevail against it.'
Behold at its source the colossal inscription round the
dome of St. Peter's : *Tu es Petrus, et super hanc petram
ædificabo ecclesiam meam!*

The practical lesson to be drawn from all this is, that
we should avoid violent revolution in the words and
externals of religion.   Profound sentiments are connected
with them ; they are aimed at the highest good, however
imperfectly apprehended.   Their form often gives them
beauty, the associations which cluster around them give
them always pathos and solemnity.   They are to be
used as poetry ; while at the same time to purge and
raise our view of that ideal at which they are aimed,
should be our incessant endeavour.   Else the use of
them is mere dilettantism.   We should seek, therefore, to

use them as Jesus did. How freely Jesus himself used them, we see. And yet what a difference between the meaning he put upon them and the meaning put upon them by the Jews! In how general a sense alone can it with truth be said, that he and even his disciples had the same aspirations, the same final aim! How imperfectly did his disciples apprehend him; how imperfectly must they have reported him! But the result has justified his way of proceeding. For while he carried with him, so
• far as was possible, his disciples, and the world after them, and all who even now see him through the eyes of those first generations, he yet also marked his own real meaning so indelibly, that it shows and shines clearly out, to satisfy all whom,—as time goes on, and experience widens, and more things are known,—the old imperfect apprehension dissatisfies. And it is not to be supposed that a rejection of all the poetry of popular religion is necessary or advisable now, any more than when Jesus came. But it is an aim which may well indeed be pursued with enthusiasm, to make the true meaning of Jesus, in using that poetry, emerge and prevail. For the immense pathos, so perpetually enlarged upon, of his life and death, does really culminate here : that Christians have so profoundly misunderstood him.

And perhaps I may seem to have said in this essay

a great deal about what was merely poetry to Jesus, but too little about what was his real meaning. What this was, however, I have tried to bring out elsewhere. Yet for fear, from my silence about it here, this essay should seem to want due balance, let me end with what a man who writes it down for himself, and meditates on it, and entitles it *Christ's religion*, will not, perhaps, go far wrong. It is but a series of well-known sayings of Jesus himself, as the Gospels deliver them to us. But by putting them together in the following way, and by connecting them, we enable ourselves, I think, to understand better both what Jesus himself meant, and how his disciples came with ease,—taking the sayings singly and interpreting them by the light of their preconceptions,—to mistake them. We must begin, surely, with that wherewith both he and they began ;—with that wherewith Christianity itself begins, and wherein it ends : 'the kingdom of God.'

*The time is fulfilled and the kingdom of God is at hand ! change the inner man and believe the good news !*

*He that believeth hath eternal life. He that heareth my word, and believeth him that sent me, hath eternal life, and cometh not into judgment, but hath passed from death to life. Verily, verily, I say unto you, The hour cometh*

*and now is, when the dead shall hear the voice of the Son
of God, and they that hear shall live.*

*I am come forth from God and am here, for I have not
come of myself, but he sent me. No man can come unto
me except the Father that sent me draw him; and I will
raise him up in the last day. He that is of God heareth
the words of God; my doctrine is not mine but his that
sent me. He that receiveth me receiveth him that sent
me.*

*And why call ye me Lord, Lord, and do not what I
say? If ye know these things, happy are ye if ye* do *them.
Cleanse that which is* within; *the evil thoughts from
within, from the heart,* they *defile the man. And why
seest thou the mote that is in thy brother's eye, but perceivest
not the beam that is in thine own eye? Take heed to your-
selves against insincerity; God knoweth your hearts;
blessed are the pure in heart, for they shall see God!*

*Come unto me, all that labour and are heavy-burdened,
and I will give you rest. Take my yoke upon you, and
learn of me that I am mild and lowly in heart, and ye
shall find rest unto your souls. For my yoke is kindly,
and my burden light.*

*I am the bread of life; he that cometh to me shall never
hunger, and he that believeth on me shall never thirst. I*

am the living bread; as the living Father sent me, and I live by the Father, so he that eateth me, even he shall live by me. It is the spirit that maketh live, the flesh profiteth nothing; the words which I have said unto you, they are spirit and they are life. If a man keep my word, he shall never see death. My sheep hear my voice, and I know them, and they follow me, and I give unto them eternal life, and they shall never perish.

If a man serve me, let him follow me; and where I am, there shall also my servant be. Whosoever doth not carry his cross and come after me, cannot be my disciple. If any man will come after me, let him renounce himself, and take up his cross daily, and follow me. For whosoever will save his life shall lose it; but whosoever shall lose his life for my sake and the sake of the good news, the same shall save it. For what is a man profited, if he gain the whole world, but lose himself, be mulcted of himself? Therefore doth my Father love me, because I lay down my life that I may take it again. A new commandment give I unto you, that ye love one another. The Son of man came not to be served but to serve, and to give his life a ransom for many.

I am the resurrection and the life; he that believeth on me, though he die, shall live; and he that liveth and believeth on me shall never die. I am come that ye might *have life, and that ye might have it more abundantly. I cast out devils and I do cures to-day and to-morrow; and the third day I shall be perfected. Yet a little while, and the world seeth me no more; but ye see me, because I live and ye shall live. If ye keep my commandments ye shall abide in my love, like as I have kept my Father's commandments and abide in his love. He that loveth me shall be loved of my Father, and I will love him, and will manifest myself to him. If a man love me, he will keep my word, and my Father will love him, and we will come unto him, and make our abode with him.*

*I am the good shepherd; the good shepherd lays down his life for the sheep. And other sheep I have, which are not of this fold; them also must I bring, and they shall be one flock, one shepherd. Fear not, little flock, for it is your Father's good pleasure to give you the kingdom.*

*My kingdom is not of this world; the kingdom of God cometh not with observation; behold, the kingdom of God is within you! Whereunto shall I liken the kingdom of God? It is like a grain of mustard seed, which a man took and cast into his garden, and it grew, and waxed a great tree, and the fowls of the air lodged in the branches of it. It is like leaven, which a woman took, and hid in three measures of meal, till the whole was leavened. So is the kingdom of God, as a man may cast seed in the ground, and may go to bed and get up night and day, and the seed shoots and extends he knoweth not how.*

*And this good news of the kingdom shall be preached in the whole world, for a witness to all nations; and then shall the end come.*

With such a construction in his thoughts to govern his use of it, Jesus loved and freely adopted the common wording and imagery of the popular Jewish religion.   In dealing with the popular religion in which we have been ourselves bred, we may the more readily follow his example, inasmuch as, though all error has its side of moral danger, yet, evidently, the misconception of their religion by Christians has produced no such grave moral perversion as we see to have been produced in the Scribes and Pharisees by their misconception of the religion of the Old Testament.   The fault of popular Christianity as an endeavour after *righteousness by Jesus Christ* is not, like the fault of popular Judaism as an endeavour after *salvation by righteousness*, first and foremost a moral fault.   It is, much more, an intellectual one. But it is not on that account insignificant.   Dr. Mozley urges, that 'no inquiry is obligatory upon religious minds in matters of the supernatural and miraculous,' because, says he, though 'the human mind must refuse to submit to anything contrary to moral sense in Scripture,' yet 'there is no moral question raised by the fact of a miracle, nor does a supernatural doctrine challenge any moral resistance.' As if there were no possible resistance to religious doctrines, but a resistance on the ground of their immorality ! As if intellectual resistance to them counted for nothing ! The objections to popular Christianity are not moral objections, but intellectual revolt against its demonstrations by miracle and metaphysics. To be intellectually convinced of a thing's want of conformity to truth and fact is surely an insuperable obstacle to receiving it, even though there be no moral obstacle added. And no moral advantages of a doctrine can avail to save it, in presence of the intellectual conviction of its want of conformity with truth and fact. And if the want of conformity exists, it is sure to be one day found out. 'Things are what they are, and the consequences of them will be what they will be ; ' and one inevitable consequence of a thing's want of conformity with truth and fact is, that sooner or later the human mind perceives it. And whoever thinks that the ground-belief of Christians is true and indispensable, but that in the account they give of it, and of the reasons for holding it, there is a want of conformity with truth and fact, may well desire to find a better account and better reasons, and to

prepare the way for their admission and for their acquiring some strength and consistency in men's minds,
against the day when the old means of reliance fail.

But, meanwhile, the ground-belief of all Christians,
whatever account they may give to themselves of its
source and sanctions, is in itself an indestructible basis of
fellowship.   Whoever believes the final triumph of Christianity, the Christianisation of the world, to have all the
necessity and grandeur of a natural law, will never lack a
bond of profound sympathy with popular religion.
Compared with agreement and difference on this point,
agreement and difference on other points seem trifling.
To believe that, whoever are ignorant that righteousness
is salvation, ' the Eternal shall have them in derision ;' to
believe that, whatever may be the substitute offered for the
righteousness of Jesus, a substitute however sparkling,
yet ' whosoever drinketh of *this* water shall thirst again ; '
to desire truly ' to have strength to escape all the things
which shall come to pass and to stand before the Son of
Man,'—is the one authentic mark and seal of the household
of faith.   Those who share in this belief and in this desire
are fellow-citizens of the ' city which hath foundations.'
Whosoever shares in them not, is, or is in danger of any
day becoming, a wanderer, as St. Augustine says, through
' the waste places fertile in sorrow ;' a wanderer ' seeking

rest and finding none.' *In all things I sought rest; then the Creator of all things gave me commandment and said: Let thy·dwelling be in Jacob, and thine inheritance in Israel! And so was I established in Sion; likewise in the beloved city he gave me rest, and in Jerusalem was my power.*

## *BISHOP BUTLER AND THE ZEIT-GEIST.*[1]

### I.

IN Scotland, I imagine, you have in your philosophical studies small experience of the reverent devotion formerly, at any rate, paid at Oxford to text-books in philosophy, such as the *Sermons* of Bishop Butler, or the *Ethics* of Aristotle. Your students in philosophy have always read pretty widely, and have not concentrated themselves, as we at Oxford used to concentrate ourselves, upon one or two great books. However, in your study of the Bible you got abundant experience of our attitude of mind towards our two philosophers. Your text-book was right; there were no mistakes *there*. If there was anything obscure, anything hard to be comprehended, it was

[1] The two following discourses were delivered as lectures at the Edinburgh Philosophical Institution. They had the form, therefore, of an address to hearers, not readers; and they are printed in that form in which they were delivered.

your ignorance which was in fault, your failure of comprehension. Just such was our mode of dealing with Butler's
*Sermons* and Aristotle's *Ethics.* Whatever was hard,
whatever was obscure, the text-book was all right, and our
understandings were to conform themselves to it. What
agonies of puzzle has Butler's account of self-love, or
Aristotle's of the intellectual virtues, caused to clever
undergraduates and to clever tutors ; and by what feats
of astonishing explanation, astonishingly acquiesced in,
were those agonies calmed ! Yet the true solution of
the difficulty was in some cases, undoubtedly, that our
author, as he stood, was not right, not satisfactory. As
to secular authors, at any rate, it is indisputable that their
works are to be regarded as contributions to human
knowledge, and not more. It is only experience which
assures us that even the poetry and artistic form of
certain epochs has not, in fact, been improved upon, and
is, therefore, classical. But the same experience assures
us that in all matters of knowledge properly so called,—
above all, of such difficult knowledge as are questions of
mind and of moral philosophy,—any writer in past times
must be on many points capable of correction, much of
what he says must be capable of being put more truly,
put clearer. Yet we at Oxford used to read our Aristotle
or our Butler with the same absolute faith in the classi-

cality of their matter as in the classicality of Homer's
form.

The time inevitably arrives, to people who think at all
seriously, when, as their experience widens, they ask
themselves what they are really to conclude about the
masters and the works thus authoritatively imposed upon
them in their youth. Above all, of a man like Butler one
is sure to ask oneself this,—an Englishman, a Christian,
a modern, whose circumstances and point of view we
can come pretty well to know and to understand, and
whose works we can be sure of possessing just as he
published them and meant them to stand before us.
And Butler deserves that one should regard him very
attentively, both on his own account, and also because of
the immense and confident laudation bestowed upon his
writings. Whether he completely satisfies us or no, a
man so profoundly convinced that 'virtue,—the law of
virtue written on our hearts,—is the law we are born
under ; ' a man so staunch in his respectful allegiance to
reason, a man who says : ' I express myself with caution,
lest I should be mistaken to vilify reason, which is indeed ·
the only faculty we have wherewith to judge concerning anything, even revelation itself ; ' a man, finally, so
deeply and evidently in earnest, filled with so awful a
sense of the reality of things and of the madness of self-

deception : 'Things and actions are what they are, and
the consequences of them will be what they will be ;
why then should we desire to be deceived?'—such a
man, even if he was somewhat despotically imposed upon
our youth, may yet well challenge the most grave consideration from our mature manhood. And even did we
fail to give it willingly, the strong consenting eulogy
upon his achievements would extort it from us. It is
asserted that his three Sermons on Human Nature are, in
the department of moral philosophy, ' perhaps the three
most valuable essays that were ever published.' They
are this, because they contain his famous doctrine of
conscience,—a doctrine which, being in those sermons
' explained according to the strict truth of our mental constitution, is irresistible.' Butler is therefore said, in the
words of another of his admirers, ' by pursuing precisely
the same mode of reasoning in the science of morals as
his great predecessor Newton had done in the system of
nature, to have formed and concluded a happy alliance
between faith and philosophy.' And again : 'Metaphysic, which all then had nothing to support it but mere
abstraction or shadowy speculation, Butler placed on the
firm basis of observation and experiment.' And Sir James
Mackintosh says of the *Sermons* in general : ' In these
sermons Butler has taught truths more capable of being

F

exactly distinguished from the doctrines of his predecessors, more satisfactorily established by him, more
comprehensively applied to particulars, more rationally
connected with each other, and therefore more worthy
of the name of *discovery*, than any with which we are
acquainted, if we ought not, with some hesitation, to
except the first steps of the Grecian philosophers towards
a theory of morals.' The *Analogy* Mackintosh calls
' the most original and profound work extant in any
language on the philosophy of religion.' Such are
Butler's claims upon our attention.

It is true, there are moments when the philosophy of
religion and the theory of morals are not popular subjects,
when men seem disposed to put them out of their minds,
to shelve them as sterile, to try whether they cannot get
on without them. Mr. John Morley, in that interesting
series of articles on Diderot which he has lately published
in the *Fortnightly Review*, points out how characteristic
and popular in the French Encyclopædia was its authors'
' earnest enthusiasm for all the purposes, intents, and
details of productive industry, for physical science and the
practical arts ; ' how this was felt to be a welcome relief
to people tired of metaphysical and religious discussions.
' Intellectually,' says he, ' it was the substitution of interest
in things for interest in words.' And undoubtedly

there are times when a reaction of this sort sets in, when an interest in the processes of productive industry, in physical science and the practical arts, is called *an interest in things*, and an interest in morals and religion is called *an interest in words.* People really do seem to imagine that in seeing and learning how buttons are made, or *papier mâché*, they shall find some new and untried vital resource ; that our prospects from this sort of study have something peculiarly hopeful and animating about them, and that the positive and practical thing to do is to give up religion and turn to them. However, as Butler says in his sermon on Self-Deceit : ' Religion is true, or it is not. If it be not, there is no reason for any concern about it.' If, however, it be true, it is important, and then it requires attention ; as in the same sermon Butler says, in his serious way : ' We cannot be acquainted with, nor in any propriety of speech be said to know, anything but what we attend to.' And he speaks of the disregard of men for what he calls ' the reproofs and instructions' that they meet with in religion and morals, as a disregard of what is ' exactly suitable to the state of their own mind and the course of their behaviour ; '—more suitable, he would certainly have thought, than being instructed how buttons are made, or *papier mâché.* I am entirely of Butler's opinion. And

F 2

though the posture of mind of a good many clever
persons at the present day is that of the French Ency-
clopædists, yet here in the capital of Scotland, of that
country which has been such a stronghold of what I call
' Hebraism,' of deep and ardent occupation with righteousness and religion, you will not complain of my taking for
my subject so eminent a doctor in the science of these
matters as Butler, and one who is said to have established his doctrine so firmly and impregnably. I can
conceive no claim more great to advance on a man's
behalf, and none which it more behoves us to test accu-
rately. Let us attempt to satisfy ourselves how far, in
Butler's case, the claim is solid.

### 2.

But first we should have before our minds a notion
of the life and circumstances of the man with whose
works we are going to deal. Joseph Butler was born on
the 18th of May, 1692, at Wantage, in Berkshire. His
father was a retired tradesman, a Dissenter, and the son
was sent to a Dissenting school. Even before he left
school, he had his first correspondence with Dr. Samuel
Clarke on certain points in Clarke's *Demonstration of the
Being and Attributes of God*, and he wrote to a friend
that he ' designed to make truth the business of his life.'

Dissent did not satisfy him. He left the Presbyterian body, to which his father belonged, and was entered, in 1714, at Oxford, at Oriel College. There he formed a friendship with Edward Talbot, a Fellow of Oriel, son of Bishop Talbot, and brother to the future Lord Chancellor Talbot ; and this friendship determined the outward course of Butler's life. It led to his being appointed preacher at the Rolls Chapel, in 1719, the year after his ordination as priest, and when he was only twenty-six years old. There the famous Sermons were preached, between 1719 and 1726. Bishop Talbot appointed him, in 1722, to the living of Haughton, in the diocese of Durham ; and, in 1725, transferred him to the rich living of Stanhope, in the same diocese. After obtaining Stanhope, Butler resigned, in 1726, his preachership at the Rolls, and published his Fifteen Sermons. They made no noise. It was four years before a second edition of them was re-quired. Butler, however, had friends who knew his worth, and in 1733 he was made chaplain to Lord Chancellor Talbot, in 1736 Clerk of the Closet to Queen Caroline, the wife of George the Second. In this year he published the *Analogy.* Queen Caroline died the year afterwards, and Butler returned to Stanhope. But Queen Caroline had, before her death, strongly recommended him to her husband ; and George the Second, in 1738, made him

Bishop of Bristol, then the poorest of sees, with an income of but some 400*l.* a year. About eighteen months afterwards, Butler was appointed to the deanery of St. Paul's, when he resigned Stanhope and passed his time between Bristol and London, acquiring a house at Hampstead. He attended the House of Lords regularly, but took no part, so far as is known, in the debates. In 1746 he was made Clerk of the Closet to the King, and in 1750 he was translated to the great and rich see of Durham. Butler's health had by this time given way. In 1751 he delivered his first and only charge to the clergy of Durham, the famous Charge upon the *Use and Importance of External Religion.* But in June, 1752, he was taken in a state of extreme weakness to Bath, died there on the 16th of June, and was buried in his old cathedral of Bristol. When he died, he was just sixty years of age. He was never married.

Such are, in outline, the external facts of Butler's life and history. To fill up the outline for us there remain a very few anecdotes, and one or two letters. Bishop Philpotts, of Exeter, who afterwards followed Butler in the living of Stanhope, sought eagerly at Stanhope for some traditions of his great predecessor. All he could gather was, that Butler had been much beloved, that he rode about on a black pony and rode very fast,

and that he was greatly pestered by beggars because of
his known easiness. But there has been preserved
Butler's letter to Sir Robert Walpole on accepting the
see of Bristol, and a passage in this letter is curious, as
coming from such a man. He expresses his gratitude to
the King, and then proceeds thus :—

I know no greater obligation than to find the Queen's con-
descending goodness and kind intentions towards me transferred to his Majesty. Nor is it possible, while I live, to be
without the most grateful sense of his favour to me, whether
the effects of it be greater or less ; for this must, in some
measures, depend upon accident. Indeed, the bishopric of
Bristol is not very suitable either to the condition of my
fortune or the circumstances, nor, as I should have thought,
answerable to the recommendation with which I was honoured.
But you will excuse me, sir, if I think of this last with greater
sensibility than the conduct of affairs will admit of. But
without entering further into detail, I desire, sir, you will
please let his Majesty know that I humbly accept this instance
of his favour with the utmost possible gratitude.

As one reads that passage, it is impossible not to
have the feeling that we are in the somewhat arid air of
the eighteenth century. Ken or Leighton, in the seventeenth century, could not have written it ; and in Butler's
own century that survivor of the saints, Wilson of Sodor
and Man, could not have written it. And indeed the
peculiar delicacy and loveliness which attaches to our

idea of a saint does not belong to Butler. Nobly
severe with himself he was, his eye was single. Austerely
just, he follows with awe-filled observance the way of
duty;—this is his stamp of character. And his liberality
and his treatment of patronage, even though we may not
find in him the delicacy of the saint, are yet thorough
and admirable because they are determined by this
character. He said to his secretary : 'I should be
ashamed of myself if I could leave ten thousand pounds
behind me.' There is a story of a man coming to him
at Durham with a project for some good work. The
plan struck Butler's mind ; he sent for his house-steward,
and asked him how much money there was in his hands.
The steward answered that he had five hundred pounds.
' Five hundred pounds !' said Butler, 'what a shame for a
bishop to have so much money ! Give it away, give it all
to this gentleman for his charitable plan !' Open house
and plain living were Butler's rule at Durham. He had
long been disgusted, he said, with the fashionable expense
of time and money in entertainments, and was determined
it should receive no countenance from his example. He
writes to one who congratulated him on his translation to
Durham : ' If one is enabled to do a little good, and to
prefer worthy men, this indeed is a valuable of life, and
will afford satisfaction at the close of it ; but the station

of itself will in nowise answer the trouble of it, and of
getting into new forms of living ; I mean in respect to
the peace and happiness of one's own mind, for in
fortune to be sure it will.' Again one has a sense, from
something in the phraseology and mode of expression,
that one is in the eighteenth century ; but at the same
time what a perfect impression of integrity and simplicity
do Butler's words leave ! To another congratulator he
writes :—

I thank you for your kind congratulations, though I am
not without my doubts and fears how far the occasion of
them is a real subject of congratulation to me. Increase of
fortune is insignificant to one who thought he had enough
before ; and I foresee many difficulties in the station I am
coming into, and no advantage worth thinking of, except
some greater power of being serviceable to others ; and
whether this be an advantage depends entirely on the use
one shall make of it ; I pray God it may be a good one. It
would be a melancholy thing, in the close of life, to have no
reflexions to entertain oneself with but that one had spent
the revenues of the bishopric of Durham in a sumptuous
course of living, and enriched one's friends with the pro-
motions of it, instead of having really set oneself to do good,
and promote worthy men ; yet this right use of fortune and
power is more difficult than the generality of even good
people think, and requires both a guard upon oneself, and
a strength of mind to withstand solicitations, greater (I wish
I may not find it) than I am master of.

There are not half a dozen of Butler's private letters

preserved. It was worth while, therefore, to quote his letter to Walpole; and it was but just, after quoting that letter, to quote this to his congratulators.

Like Bishop Philpotts, one may well be tantalised at not knowing more of a man so full of purpose, and who has made his mark so deeply. Butler himself, however, helped to baffle us. The codicil to his will, made in 1752, not two months before his death, concludes thus :—' It is my positive and express will, that all my sermons, letters, and papers whatever, which are in a deal box, locked, directed to Dr. Forster, and now standing in the little room within my library at Hampstead, be burnt without being read by any one, as soon as may be after my decease.' His silent, inward, concentrated nature pondered well and decided what it meant to give to the world ;—gave it, and would give no more. A characteristic habit is mentioned of him, that he loved to walk alone, and to walk at night. He was an immense reader. It is said of him that he read every book he could lay his hands upon ; but it was all digested silently, not exhibited in the way of extract and citation. Unlike the seventeenth century divines, he hardly ever quotes. As to his tastes and habits, we are informed, further, that he was fond of religious music, and took for his under-secretary an ex-chorister of St.

Paul's, that he might play to him upon the organ. He liked building and planting, and one of his few letters preserved bears witness to these tastes, and is altogether so characteristic, and, in the paucity of records concerning Butler, so valuable, that I will quote it. It is to the Duchess of Somerset, and written in 1751, just after he had taken possession of the see of Durham : —

I had a mind to see Auckland before I wrote to your Grace ; and as you take so kind a part in everything which contributes to my satisfaction, I am sure you will be pleased to hear that the place is a very agreeable one, and fully answering expectations, except that one of the chief prospects, which is very pretty (the river Wear, with hills much diversified rising above it), is too bare of wood ; the park, not much amiss as to that, but I am obliged to pale it anew all round, the old pale being quite decayed. This will give an opportunity, with which I am much pleased, to take in forty or fifty acres completely wooded, though with that enlargement it will scarce be sufficient for the hospitality of the country. These, with some little improvements and very great repairs, take up my leisure time.

Thus, madam, I seem to have laid out a very long life for myself ; yet, in reality, everything I see puts me in mind of the shortness and uncertainty of it : the arms and inscriptions of my predecessors, what they did and what they neglected, and (from accidental circumstances) the very place itself, and the rooms I walk through and sit in. And when I consider, in one view, the many things of the kind I have just mentioned which I have upon my hands, I feel the burlesque of being employed in this manner at my time of life. But in another

view, and taking in all circumstances, these things, as trifling
as they may appear, no less than things of greater importance,
seem to be put upon me to do, or at least to begin ; whether
I am to live to complete any or all of them, is not my concern.

With Butler's taste for building and improving is
connected a notable incident.  While at Bristol he
restored the episcopal palace and chapel, and in the
chapel he put up an altar-piece, which is described as
' of black marble, inlaid with a milk-white cross of white
marble, which is plain, and has a good effect.'   For
those bare Hanoverian times this was a reredos case.
Butler's cross excited astonishment and gave offence, and
Lord Chancellor Hardwicke begged a subsequent Bishop
of Bristol, Dr. Young, to have it taken down.   Young
made the excellent answer, that it should never be said
that Bishop Young had pulled down what Bishop Butler
had set up ; and the cross remained until the palace was
burnt and the marble altar-piece destroyed in the Bristol
riots in 1831.   But the erection of this cross was connected with his remarks, in his Durham Charge, on the
*Use and Importance of External Religion*, and caused it to
be reported that Butler had died in the communion of the
Church of Rome.   Pamphleteers and newspaper-writers
handled the topic in the style which we know so well.
Archbishop Secker thought it necessary to write in denial

of his friend's perversion, owning, as he did so, that for
himself he wished the cross had not been put up. And
Butler's accuser replied, as ' Phileleutheros,' to Secker,
that ' such anecdote had been given him, and that he was
yet of opinion there is not anything improbable in it,
when it is considered that the same prelate put up the
Popish insignia of the cross in his chapel, when at
Bristol ; and in his last episcopal charge has squinted
very much towards that superstition.' Another writer not
only maintained that the cross and the Durham charge together ' amounted to full proof of a strong attachment to
the idolatrous communion of the Church of Rome,' but
volunteered to account for Butler's ' tendency this way,'
as he called it. This he did ' from the natural melancholy and gloominess of Dr. Butler's disposition, from
his great fondness for the lives of Romish saints, and
their books of mystic piety ; from his drawing his notions
of teaching men religion, not from the New Testament,
but from philosophical and political opinions of his own ;
and, above all, from his transition from a strict Dissenter
amongst the Presbyterians to a rigid Churchman, and his
sudden and unexpected elevation to great wealth and
dignity in the Church.' It was impossible that Butler
should be understood by the ordinary religious world
of his own day. But no intelligent man can now read

the Durham charge without feeling that its utterer lives
in a higher world than that in which disputes between
Catholicism and Protestantism, and questions of going
over to Rome, or at any rate 'squinting very much
towards that superstition,' have their being.  Butler
speaks as a man with an awful sense of religion, yet
plainly seeing, as he says, 'the deplorable distinction' of
his own age to be ' an avowed scorn of religion in some,
and a growing disregard to it in the generality.'  He
speaks, with 'the immoral thoughtlessness,' as he called
it, of the bulk of mankind astounding and grieving his
soul, and with the single desire ' to beget a practical
sense of religion upon their hearts.'   'The form of
religion,' he says, with his invincible sense for reality,
' may indeed be where there is little of the thing itself ;
but the thing itself cannot be preserved amongst mankind without the form.'   And the form he exhorts to is
no more than what nowadays all religious people would
think matter of course to be practised, and where not
practised, to be enjoined : family prayer, grace at meals,
that the clergy should visit their parishioners and should
lay hold of natural opportunities, such as confirmation
or sickness, for serious conversation with them and for
turning their thoughts towards religion.

Butler met John Wesley, and one would like to have a

full record of what passed at such a meeting. But all that
we know is this : that when Butler was at Bristol, Wesley,
who admired the *Analogy*, and who was then preaching
to the Kingswood miners, had an interview with him ;
and that Butler 'expressed his pleasure at the seriousness
which Wesley's preaching awakened, but blamed him for
sanctioning that violent physical excitement which was
considered almost a necessary part of the so-called new
birth.'

I have kept for the last the description we have from
Surtees, the historian of Durham, of Butler's person and
manners :—

' During the short time that he held the see,' says Surtees,
' he conciliated all hearts. In advanced years and on the
episcopal throne, he retained the same genuine modesty and
native sweetness of disposition which had distinguished him
in youth and in retirement. During the ministerial performance of the sacred office, a divine animation seemed to
pervade his whole manner, and lighted up his pale, wan
countenance, already marked with the progress of disease.'

From another source we hear :—

He was of a most reverend aspect ;—his face thin and
pale, but there was a divine placidness in his countenance,
which inspired veneration and expressed the most benevolent
mind. His white hair hung gracefully on his shoulders, and
his whole figure was patriarchal.

This description would not ill suit Wesley himself, and

it may be thought, perhaps, that here at any rate, if not in the letter to Sir Robert Walpole, we find the saint. And, doubtless, where the eye is so single and the thoughts are so chastened as they were with Butler, the saintly character will never be far off. But still the total impression left by Butler is not exactly, I repeat, that of a saint.

Butler stood alone in his time and amongst his generation. Yet the most cursory reader can perceive that, in his writings, there is constant reference to the controversies of his time, and to the men of his generation. He himself has pointed this out as a possible cause of obscurity. In the preface to the second edition of his Sermons he says :—

A subject may be treated in a manner which all along supposes the reader acquainted with what has been said upon it both by ancient and modern writers, and with what is the present state of opinion in the world concerning such subject. This will create a difficulty of a very peculiar kind, and even throw an obscurity over the whole before those who are not thus informed ; but those who are, will be disposed to excuse such a manner, and other things of the like kind, as a saving of their patience.

This reference to contemporary opinion, if it sometimes occasions difficulty in following Butler, makes his treatment of his subject more real and earnest. Nearly always he has in mind something with which he has

actually come in conflict. When he recurs so persist-
ently to self-love, he is thinking of the ' strange affectation
in many people of explaining away all particular affections, and representing the whole of life as nothing but
one continual exercise of self-love,' by which he had so
often been made impatient. One of the signal merits of
Mr. Pattison's admirable sketch, in *Essays and Reviews*,
of the course of religious ideas in England from the Revolution to the middle of the eighteenth century, is that it
so clearly marks this correspondence, at the time when
Butler wrote, between what English society argued and
what English theology answered. Society was full of discussions about religion, of objections to eternal punishment as inconsistent with the Divine goodness, and to a
system of future rewards as subversive of a disinterested
love of virtue :—

'The deistical writers,' says Mr. Pattison, 'formed the
atmosphere which educated people breathed. The objections
the *Analogy* meets are not new and unreasoned objections,
but such as had worn well, and had borne the rub of con-
troversy, because they were genuine. It was in society, and
not in his study, that Butler had learned the weight of the
deistical arguments.'

And in a further sentence Mr. Pattison, in my opinion,
has almost certainly put his finger on the very determining
cause of the *Analogy's* existence :—

At the Queen's philosophical parties, where these topics
(the deistical objections) were canvassed with earnestness
and freedom, Butler must often have felt the impotence of
reply in detail, and seen, as he says, ' how impossible it must
be, in a cursory conversation, to unite all into one argument,
and represent it as it ought to be.'

This connecting of the *Analogy* with the Queen's
philosophical parties seems to me an idea inspired by
true critical genius. The parties given by Queen Caroline,—a clever and strong-minded woman,—the recluse
and grave Butler had, as her Clerk of the Closet, to
attend regularly. Discussion was free at them, and there
Butler no doubt heard in abundance the talk of what is
well described as the 'loose kind of deism which was
the then tone of fashionable circles.' The *Analogy*,
with its peculiar strain and temper, is the result. ' Cavil-
ling and objecting upon any subject is much easier than
clearing up difficulties ; and this last part will always be
put upon the defenders of religion.' Surely that must be
a reminiscence of the 'loose kind of deism' and of its
maintainers ! And then comes the very sentence which
Mr. Pattison has in part quoted, and which is worth
quoting entire :—

Then, again, the general evidence of religion is complex
and various. It consists of a long series of things, one pre-
paratory and confirming another, from the very beginning of

the world to the present time. And 'tis easy to see how impossible it must be, in a cursory conversation, to unite all this into one argument and represent it as it ought ; and, could it be done, how utterly indisposed people would be to attend to it. I say in a cursory conversation, whereas unconnected objections are thrown out in a few words and are easily apprehended, without more attention than is usual in common talk. So that notwithstanding we have the best cause in the world, and though a man were very capable of defending it, yet I know not why he should be forward to undertake it upon so great a disadvantage and to so little good effect, as it must be done amidst the gaiety and carelessness of common conversation.

In those remarks to the Durham clergy, Butler, I say again, was surely thinking of difficulties with which he had himself wrestled, and of which the remembrance made the strenuous tone of his *Analogy,* as he laboured at it, yet more strenuous. What a *sæva indignatio* burns in the following passage from the conclusion to that work :—

Let us suppose that the evidence of religion in general, and of Christianity, has been seriously inquired into by all reasonable men among us. Yet we find many professedly to reject both, upon speculative principles of infidelity. And all of them do not content themselves with a bare neglect of religion, and enjoying their imaginary freedom from its restraints. Some go much beyond this. They deride God's moral government over the world. They renounce his protection and defy his justice. They ridicule and vilify

Christianity, and blaspheme the Author of it ; and take all occasions to manifest a scorn and contempt of revelation. This amounts to an active setting themselves against religion, to what may be considered as a positive principle of irreligion, which they cultivate within themselves, and, whether they intend this effect or not, render habitual, as a good man does the contrary principle. And others, who are not chargeable with all this profligateness, yet are in avowed opposition to religion, as if discovered to be groundless.

And with the same penetrating tone of one who has seen with his own eyes that of which he complains, has heard it with his own ears, suffered from it in his own person, Butler, in 1740, talks of 'the dark prospects before us from that profligateness of manners and scorn of religion which so generally abound;' and, in 1751, speaking in the last year but one of his life, he thus begins his charge to the clergy of Durham :—

It is impossible for me, my brethren, upon our first meeting of this kind, to forbear lamenting with you the general decay of religion in this nation, which is now observed by everyone, and has been for some time the complaint of all serious persons. The influence of it is more and more wearing out of the minds of men, even of those who do not pretend to enter into speculations upon the subject. But the number of those who do, and who profess themselves unbelievers, increases, and with their numbers their zeal.

One cannot but ask oneself, when one considers the steadiness of our country through the French Revolution.

when one considers the power and prevalence of religion,
even after every deduction has been made for what
impairs its strength,—the power and prevalence, I say, of
religion in our country at this hour,—one cannot but ask
oneself whether Butler was not over-desponding, whether
he saw the whole real state of things, whether he did not
attach over-importance to certain workings which he did
see.   Granted that he himself did something to cure the
evil which he describes ; granted that others did something.   Yet, had the evil existed fully as he describes it,
I doubt whether he, and Wesley, and all the other phy-
sicians, could have cured it.   I doubt, even, whether
their effort would itself have been possible.   Look at a
contemporary of Butler in France,—a man who, more
than any one else, reminds me of Butler,—the great
French statesman, the greatest, in my opinion, that
France has ever had ; look at Turgot.   Turgot was like
Butler in his mental energy, in his deep moral and intellectual ardour, his strenuousness.   ' Every science, every
language, every literature, every business,' says Michelet,
' interested Turgot.'   But that in which Turgot most
resembled Butler was what Michelet calls his *férocité*,—
what I should rather call his *sæva indignatio*.   Like
Butler, Turgot was filled with an astonished, awful,
oppressive sense of ' the immoral thoughtlessness ' of

men ; of the heedless, hazardous way in which they
deal with things of the greatest moment to them ; of
the immense, incalculable misery which is due to this
cause. 'The greatest evils in life,' Turgot held, just as
Butler did, 'have had their rise from somewhat which
was thought of too little importance to be attended to.'
And for these serious natures religion, one would think,
is the line of labour which would naturally first suggest
itself. And Turgot was destined for the Church ; he
prepared to take orders, like Butler. But in 1752, when
Butler lay dying at Bath, Turgot,—the true spiritual yoke-
fellow of Butler, with Butler's sacred horror at men's
frivolity, with Butler's sacred ardour for rescuing them
from the consequences of it,—Turgot, at the age of
twenty-five, could stand religion, as in France religion then
presented itself to him, no longer. ' *Il jeta ce masque*,'
says Michelet, adopting an expression of Turgot's own ;
'he flung away that mask.' He took to the work of
civil government ; in what spirit we many of us know,
and whoever of us does not know should make it his
business to learn. Nine years afterwards began his
glorious administration as Intendant of the Limousin, in
which for thirteen years he showed what manner of spirit
he was of. When, in 1774, he became Minister and
Controller-General, he showed the same thing on a more

conspicuous stage. 'Whatsoever things are true, whatsoever things are nobly serious, whatsoever things are
just, whatsoever things are pure, whatsoever things are
of good report,'—that is the history of Turgot's administration ! He was a Joseph Butler in government.
True, his work, though done as secular administration,
has in fact and reality a religious character ; all work
like his has a religious character. But the point to seize
is here : that in our country, in the middle of the
eighteenth century, a man like Butler is still possible in
religion ; in France he is only possible in civil govern
ment. And that is what I call a true ' decay of religion,
the influence of it more and more wearing out of the
minds of men.' The very existence and work of Butler
proves, in spite of his own desponding words, that matters had not in his time gone so far as this in England.

But indeed Mr. Pattison, in the admirable essay
which I have mentioned, supplies us with almost positive
evidence that it had not. Amongst a number of instructive quotations to show the state of religion in
England between 1700 and 1750, Mr. Pattison gives an
extract from a violent newspaper, *The Independent Whig,*
which had been attacking the clergy for their many and
great offences, and counselling them to mend their ways.
And then the article goes on :—

The High Church Popish clergy will laugh in their sleeves at this advice, and think there is folly enough yet left among the laity to support their authority ; and will hug themselves, and rejoice over the ignorance of the Universities, the stupidity of the drunken squires, the panic of the tender sex, *and the never-to-be shaken constancy of the multitude.*

The date of that extract is 1720. The language is the well-known language of Liberal friends of progress, when they speak of persons and institutions which are inconvenient to them. But it proves, to my mind,—and there is plenty cf other evidence to prove the same thing,—it proves that religion, whatever may have been the deficiencies of itself and of its friends, was nevertheless, in 1720, still a very great and serious power in this country. And certainly it did not suddenly cease to be so between 1720 and 1750.

No, Butler's mournful language has in it, one may be almost certain, something of exaggeration. To a man of Butler's seriousness the world will always afford plenty of matter for apprehension and sorrow. And to add to this were certain special circumstances of his time, peculiarly trying to an earnest dealer, such as he was, with great thoughts and great interests. There was his bitter personal experience of 'the loose kind of deism which was the tone of fashionable circles.' There was his impatience,—half contemptuous, half indignant,—of a

state of things where, as Mr. Pattison says, ' the religious
writer had now to appear at the bar of criticism,' but of
*such* criticism ! For, ' if ever there was a time,' says Mr.
Pattison, again, ' when abstract speculation was brought
down from inaccessible heights and compelled to be intelligible, it was the period from the Revolution to 1750.'
This in itself was all very good, and Butler would have
been the last man to wish it otherwise. But to whom
was abstract speculation required thus to make itself intelligible ? To the ' fashionable circles,' to the whole
multitude of loose thinkers and loose livers, who might
choose to lend half an ear for half an hour to the great
argument. ' It must gain,' we are told, ' the wits and
the town.' Hence the *sæva indignatio.*

And therefore Butler, when he gets into the pulpit,
or when he sits down at his writing-table, will have the
thing out with his adversaries. He will ' unite it all into
one argument and represent it as it ought,' and he will
fairly argue his objectors down. He will place himself
on their own ground, take their own admissions, and
will prove to them, in a manner irresistible to any fair
thinker, that they are wrong, and that they are bound to
make their life and practice, what it is not, religious.

There is a word which I have often used, and with
my use of which some of those who hear me may

possibly be familiar : the Greek word *epieikes* or *epieikeia*, meaning that which is at once reasonable and prepossessing, or ' sweet reasonableness.' The original meaning of the word *epieikes* is, that which has an air of consummate truth and likelihood, and which, by virtue of having this air, is prepossessing. And *epieikeia* is well rendered by ' sweet reasonableness,' because that which above all things has an air of truth and likelihood, that which, therefore, above all things, is prepossessing, is whatever is sweetly reasonable. You know what a power was this quality in the talkings and dealings of Jesus Christ. *Epieikeia* is the very word to characterise true Christianity. And true Christianity wins, not by an argumentative victory, not by going through a long debate with a person, examining the arguments for his case from beginning to end, and making him confess that, whether he feels disposed to yield or no, yet in fair logic and fair reason he ought to yield. No, but it puts something which tends to transform him and his practice, it puts this particular thing in such a way before a man that he feels disposed and eager to lay hold of it. And he does, therefore, lay hold of it, though without at all perceiving, very often, the whole scheme to which it belongs ; and thus his practice gets changed. This, I think, every one will admit to be Christianity's most true and characteristic way of getting people to embrace religion. Now, it is to be observed how totally unlike a way it is to Butler's, although Butler's object is the same as Christianity's : to get people to embrace religion. And the object being the same, it must strike every one that the way followed by Christianity has the advantage of a far greater effectualness than Butler's way ; since people are much more easily attracted into making a change than argued into it. However, Butler seems to think that enough has been done if it has been proved to people, in such a way as to silence their arguments on the other side, that they *ought* to make a change. For he says expressly :—

There being, as I have shown, such evidence for religion as is sufficient in reason to influence men to embrace it, to object that it is not to be imagined mankind *will* be influenced by such evidence is nothing to the purpose of the foregoing treatise (his *Analogy*). For the purpose of it is not to inquire what sort of creatures mankind are, but what the light and knowledge which is afforded them requires they should be ; to show how in reason they ought to behave, not how in fact they will behave. This depends upon themselves and is their own concern—the personal concern of each man in particular. And how little regard the generality have to it, experience, indeed, does too fully show. But religion, considered as a probation, has had its end upon all persons to whom it has been proposed with evidence sufficient in reason to influence their practice ; for by this means they have been put into a state of probation, let them behave as they will in it.

So that, in short, Butler's notion of converting the loose
deists of fashionable circles comes to this : by being
plied with evidence sufficient *in reason* to influence their
practice, they are to be put into a state of probation ; let
them behave as they will in it. Probably no one can
hear such language without a secret dissatisfaction. For,
after all, the object of religion is conversion, and to change
people's behaviour. But where, then, is the use of saying
that you will inquire not what people *are*, but how in
reason they ought to behave ? Why, it is what they *are*
which determines their sense of how they ought to behave.
Make them, therefore, so to feel what they are, as to get
a fruitful sense of how they ought to behave. The
Founder of Christianity did so ; and whatever success
Christianity has had, has been gained by this method.

However, Butler's line is what it is. We are concerned with what we can use of it. With his argumentative triumph over the loose thinkers and talkers of his
day, so far as it is a triumph won by taking their own
data and using their own admissions, we are not concerned unless their admissions and their data are ours
too. And they are not. But it is affirmed, not only that
the loose deists of fashionable circles could not answer
the *Analogy*; it is affirmed, farther, that the *Analogy* is
unanswerable. It is asserted, not only that Hobbes or
Shaftesbury delivered an unsatisfactory theory of morals,

and that Butler in his *Sermons* disputed their reasonings
with success ; but it is asserted, farther, that Butler, on his
side, 'pursued precisely the same mode of reasoning in the
science of morals as his great predecessor, Newton, had
done in the system of nature,' and that by so doing
Butler has 'formed and concluded a happy alliance
between faith and philosophy.' Achievement of this
kind is what the 'Time-Spirit,' or *Zeit-Geist*, which
sweeps away so much that is local and personal, will
certainly respect. Achievement of this sort deeply concerns us. An unanswerable work on the evidence of
religion, a science of human nature and of morals
reached by a method as sure as Newton's, a happy
alliance between faith and philosophy,—what can concern
us more deeply ? If Butler accomplished all this, he does
indeed give us what we can use ; he is indeed great. But
supposing he should turn out not to have accomplished all
this, what then ? Does he vanish away ? Does he give
us nothing which we can use ? And if he does give us
something which we can use, what is it ; and if he
remains a great man to us still, why does he ?

### 3.

Let us begin with the *Sermons at the Rolls*, Butler's
first publication. You have heard, for I have quoted it,

the unbounded praise which has been given to the three sermons *On Human Nature*. And they do indeed lay the foundation for the whole doctrine of the *Sermons at the Rolls*, of the body of sermons wherein is given Butler's system of moral philosophy. Their argument is familiar, probably, to many of us. Let me recite it briefly by abridging the best of all possible accounts of it,—Butler's own account in his preface :—

Mankind has various instincts and principles of action. The generality of mankind obey their instincts and principles, all of them, those propensions we call good as well as the bad, according to the constitution of their body and the external circumstances which they are in. They are not wholly governed by self-love, the love of power, and sensual appetites ; they are frequently influenced by friendship, compassion, gratitude ; and even a general abhorrence of what is base, and liking of what is fair and just, take their turn amongst the other motives of action. This is the partial inadequate notion of human nature treated of in the first discourse, and it is by this nature, if one may speak so, that the world is in fact influenced and kept in that tolerable order in which it is.

Mankind in thus acting would act suitably to their whole nature, if no more were to be said of man's nature than what has been now said. But that is not a complete account of man's nature. Somewhat further must be brought in to give us an adequate notion of it—namely, that one of those principles of action—*conscience* or *reflexion*—compared with the rest as they all stand together in the nature of man, plainly bears upon it marks of authority over all the rest, and claims the absolute direction of them all, to allow or forbid their gratification ; a disapprobation of reflexion being in itself a principle manifestly superior to a mere propension. And the conclusion is, that to allow no more to this superior principle or part of our nature than to other parts, to let it govern and guide only occasionally in common with the rest, as its turn happens to come, from the temper and circumstances one happens to be in—this is not to act conformably to the constitution of man, neither can any human creature be said to act conformably to his constitution and nature, unless he allows to that superior principle the absolute authority which is due to it. And this conclusion is abundantly confirmed from hence—that one may determine what course of action the economy of man's nature requires, without so much as learning in what degrees of *strength* the several principles prevail, or which of them have *actually* the greatest influence.　　　　　　　　　　　　　　　.

And the whole scope and object of the three sermons *On Human Nature*, Butler describes thus :—

They were intended to explain what is meant by the nature of man, when it is said that virtue consists in following, and vice in deviating from it ; and by explaining to show that the assertion is true.

Now, it may be at once allowed that Butler's notion of human nature as consisting of a number of instincts and principles of action, with conscience as a superior principle presiding over them, corresponds in a general way with facts of which we are all conscious, and if

practically acted upon would be found to work satisfactorily. When Butler says : ' Let any plain honest man
before he engages in any course of action, ask himself,
" Is this I am going about right, or is it wrong ?   Is it
good or is it evil ? " and I do not in the least doubt but
that this question would be answered agreeably to truth
and virtue by almost any fair man in almost any cir-
cumstance ; '—when Butler says this, he is on solid
ground, and his whole scheme has its rise, indeed, in the
sense that this ground *is* solid. When he calls our nature
' the voice of God within us ; ' or when he suggests that
there may be ' distinct from the reflexion of reason, a
mutual *sympathy* between each particular of the species,
a *fellow-feeling* common to mankind ; ' or when he finely
says of conscience, ' Had it strength as it has right, had
it power as it has manifest authority, it would absolutely
govern the world ; '—in all this, Butler is in contact with
the most precious truth and reality, and so far as this
truth and reality inform the scheme which he has drawn
out for human nature, his scheme has life in it.

Equally may it be allowed, that the errors, which his
scheme is designed to correct, are errors indeed. If the
Epicureans, or Hobbes, or any one else, ' explain the
desire of praise and of being beloved, as no other than
desire of safety ; regard to our country, even in the most

virtuous character, as nothing but regard to ourselves ;
curiosity as proceeding from interest or pride ; as if there
were no such passions in mankind as desire of esteem,
or of being beloved, or of knowledge;'—if these deli
neators of human nature represent it thus, they represent
it fantastically.   If Shaftesbury, laying it down that virtue
is the happiness of man, and encountered by the objection that one may be not convinced of this happy tendency
of virtue or may be of a contrary opinion, meets the objection by determining that the case is without remedy,
then this noble moralist moralises ill.   If Butler found
some persons (probably the loose deists of fashionable
circles) 'who, upon principle, set up for suppressing the
affection of compassion as a weakness, so that there is I
know. not what of fashion on this side, and by some
means or other the whole world, almost, is run into the
extremes of insensibility towards the distresses of their
fellow creatures ; '—if this was so, then the fashionable
theory of human nature was vicious and false, and Butler,
in seeking to substitute a better for it, was quite right.

But Butler himself brings in somebody as asking :
' Allowing that mankind hath the rule of right within
itself, what obligations are we under to attend to and
follow it ?'   And he answers this question quite fairly :
' Your obligation to obey this law, is its being the law of

H

your nature.' But let us vary the question a little, and let us ask Butler : 'Suppose your scheme of human nature to correspond in a general way, but no more, with facts of which we are conscious, and to promise to work practically well enough, what obligations are we under to attend to and follow it ? ' Butler cannot now answer us : ' Your obligation to obey this law, is its being the law of your nature.' For this is just what is not yet made out. All that we suppose to be yet made out about Butler's scheme of human nature,—its array of instincts and principles with the superior principle of conscience presiding,—is, that the scheme has a general correspondence with facts of human nature whereof we are conscious. But the time comes,—sooner or later the time comes,—to individuals and even to societies, when the foundations of the great deep are broken up, and everything is in question, and people want surer holding-ground than a sense of general correspondence, in any scheme and rule of human nature proposed to them, with facts whereof they are conscious. They ask them-selves what this sense of general correspondence is really worth. They sift the facts of which they are conscious, and their consciousness of which seemed to lend a credi-bility to the scheme proposed. They insist on strict verifi-cation of whatever is to be admitted ; and the authority of the scheme with them stands or falls according as it does or does not come out undamaged, after all this process has been gone through. If Butler's scheme of human nature comes out undamaged after being submitted to a process of this kind, then it is indeed, as its admirers call it, a Newtonian work. It is a work 'placed on the firm basis of observation and experiment ;' it is a true work of *discovery*. His doctrine may, with justice, be then called 'an irresistible doctrine made out according to the strict truth of our mental constitution.'

Let us take Butler's natural history of what he calls 'our instincts and principles of action.' It is this :—They have been implanted in us ; put into us ready-made, to serve certain ends intended by the Author of our nature. When we see what each of them 'is in itself, as placed in our nature by its Author, it will plainly appear for what ends it was placed there.' 'Perfect goodness in the Deity,' says Butler, 'is the principle from whence the universe was brought into being, and by which it is preserved ; and general benevolence is the great law of the moral creation.' But some of our passions and propensions seem to go against goodness and benevolence. However, we could not do without our stock of passions and propensions of all sorts, because 'that would leave us without a sufficient principle of action.' 'Reason alone,' argues Butler—

Reason alone, whatever any one may wish, is not in reality a sufficient motive of virtue in such a creature as man ; but this reason, joined with those affections which God has impressed upon his heart ; and when these are allowed scope to exercise themselves, but under strict government and direction of reason, then it is we act suitably to our nature, and to the circumstances God has placed us in.

And even those affections, which seem to create difficulties for us, are purposely given, Butler says—

Some of them as a guard against the violent assaults of others, and in our own defence ; some in behalf of others ; and all of them to put us upon, and help to carry us through, a course of behaviour suitable to our condition.

For—

As God Almighty foresaw the irregularities and disorders, both natural and moral, which would happen in this state of things, he hath graciously made some provision against them, by giving us several passions and affections, which arise from, or whose objects are, those disorders. Of this sort are fear, resentment, compassion, and others, of which there could be no occasion or use in a perfect state, but in the present we should be exposed to greater inconveniences without them, though there are very considerable ones which they themselves are the occasion of.

This is Butler's natural history of the origin of our

principles of action. I take leave to say that it is *not* based on observation and experiment. It is not physiology, but fanciful hypothesis. Therefore it is not Newtonian, for Newton said : *Hypotheses non fingo.* And suppose a man, in a time of great doubt and unsettlement, finding many things fail him which have been confidently pressed on his acceptance, and looking earnestly for something which he feels he can really go upon and which will prove to him a sure stay ;—suppose such a man coming to Butler, because he hears that in the ethical discussions of his sermons Butler supplies, as Mackintosh says, 'truths more satisfactorily established by him, and more worthy of the name of *discovery*, than perhaps any with which we are acquainted.' Well, such a man, I think, when he finds that Butler's ethics involve an immense hypothesis to start with, as to the origin and final causes of all our passions and affections, cannot but feel disconcerted and impatient.

And disconcerted and impatient, I am afraid, we must for the present leave him.

## BISHOP BUTLER AND THE ZEIT-GEIST.

### ' II.

BUTLER designs to found a sure system of morals, and, in order to found it, he, as we have seen, tells us how we originally came by our instincts and affections. They were, he tells us, 'placed in us by God, to put us upon and help to carry us through a course of behaviour suitable to our condition.' Here, as everyone will admit, we cannot directly verify the truth of what our author says. But he also examines such and such of our affections in themselves, to make good his theory of their origin and final causes. And here we can verify the degree in which his report of facts, and the construction he puts upon them, carries us along with it, inspires us with confidence in his scheme of human nature.

Butler notices, that compassion for the distresses of others is felt much more generally than delight in their prosperity. And he says :—

The reason and account of which matter is this : when a

man has obtained any particular advantage or felicity, his end
is gained, and he does not, in that particular, want the assistance of another ; there was therefore no need of a distinct affection towards that felicity of another already obtained, neither
would such affection directly carry him on to do good to that
person ; whereas men in distress want assistance, and compassion leads us directly to assist them. The object of the
former is the present felicity of another ; the object of the
latter is the present misery of another. It is easy to see that
the latter *wants* a particular affection for its relief, and that
the former does not want one, because it does not want
assistance.

Such an explanation, why compassion at another's distress is stronger than satisfaction at another's prosperity,
was well suited, no doubt, to Butler's theory of the origin
and final causes of all our affections. But will anyone
say that it carries a real student of nature along with
it and inspires him with confidence, any more than
Hobbes's resolution of all benevolence into a mere love
of power?—that it is not just as fantastic?

Again, take Butler's account of the passion of anger
and resentment. There is sudden anger, he says, and there
is deliberate anger :—

'The reason and the end for which man was made liable
to the passion of sudden anger is, that he might be better
qualified to prevent, and likewise (or perhaps chiefly) to
resist and defeat, sudden force, violence, and opposition,
considered merely as such. It stands in our nature for self

defence, and not for the administration of justice. Deliberate anger, on the other hand, is given us to further the ends of justice ; not natural but moral evil, not suffering but injury, raises that anger; it is resentment against vice and wickedness.

And—

The natural object of settled resentment, then, being injury, as distinct from pain or loss, it is easy to see that to prevent and to remedy such injury, and the miseries arising from it, is the end for which this passion was implanted in man.

But anger has evident dangers and abuses.    True. But—

Since it is necessary, for the very subsistence of the world, that injury, injustice, and cruelty should be punished ; and since compassion, which is so natural to mankind, would render that execution of justice exceedingly difficult and uneasy, indignation against vice and wickedness is a balance to that weakness of pity, and also to anything else which would prevent the necessary methods of severity.

And it is the business of the faculty of conscience, or reflexion, to tell us how anger may be innocently and rightly employed, so as to serve the end for which God placed it in our nature.

In times when everything is conventional, when no one looks very closely into himself or into what is told him about his moral nature, this sort of natural history may, perhaps, look likely enough, and may even pass for Newtonian. But let a time come when, as I say, the foundations of the great deep are broken up, when a man searches with passionate earnestness for something certain, and can and will henceforth build upon facts only ; then the arbitrary assertions of such a psychology as this of Butler's will be felt to be perfectly fantastic and unavailing.

And even when the arbitrary and fantastic character of his psychology is not so apparent, Butler will be felt constantly to puzzle and perplex, rather than to satisfy us. He will be felt not to carry us along with him, not to be convincing. He has his theory that our appetites and affections are all placed in our nature by God, that they are all equally natural, that they all have a useful end to serve and have respect to that end solely ; that the principle of conscience is implanted in us for the sake of arbitrating between them, of assigning to certain among them a natural superiority, of using each in its right measure and of guiding it to its right end ; and that the degree of strength, in which any one of our affections exists, affords no reason at all for following it. And Butler's theory requires, moreover, that self-love shall be but one out of our many affections, that it shall have a strictly defined end of its own, and be as distinct from those affections which seem most akin to it, and which are therefore often confounded with it, as it is from those,—such as benevolence, we will say,—which nobody is tempted to confound with it.   Such is Butler's theory, and such are its requirements.   And with this theory, we find him declaring that compassion is a primitive affection implanted in us from the first by the Author of Nature to lead us to public spirit, just as hunger was implanted in us from the first to lead us to our own personal good, and from the same cause : namely, that reason and cool self-love would not by themselves have been sufficient to lead us to the end in view, without the appetite and the affection.

The private interest of the individual would not be sufficiently provided for by reasonable and cool self-love alone ; *therefore* the appetites and passions *are placed* within as a guard and further security, without which it would not be taken due care of.   It is manifest, our life would be neglected were it not for the calls of hunger and thirst and weariness, notwithstanding that without them reason would assure us, that the recruits of food and sleep are the necessary means of our preservation.   It is therefore absurd to imagine that, without affection (the affection of compassion), the same reason alone would be more effectual to engage us to perform the duties we owe to our fellow-creatures.

The argument may be ingenious, but can anything be more unsatisfactory ?   And is it not, to use Butler's words, 'absurd to imagine' that in this manner, and by this parallel plan, and thus to supplement one another, hunger and reasonable self-love, compassion and 'a settled reasonable principle of benevolence to mankind,' did really have their rise in us?

Presently we find Butler marvelling that persons of superior capacity should dispute the obligation of compassion and public spirit, and asking if it could ever occur to a man of plain understanding to think 'that there was absolutely no such thing in mankind as affection to the good of others,—*suppose of parents to their children.*' As if the affection of parents to their children was an affection to the good of others of just the same natural history as public spirit !—as if the two were alike in their primariness, alike in their date of obligation, alike in their kind of evidence ! One is an affection of rudimentary human nature, the other is a slow conquest from rudimentary human nature. And once more :—

'To endeavour to get rid of the sorrow of compassion, by turning from the wretched, is as unnatural,' says Butler, ' as to endeavour to get rid of the pain of hunger, by keeping from the sight of food.'

Now, we are to consider this as a practical argument by which to bring a man, all unsettled about the rule of his conduct, to cultivate in himself compassion. Surely such

an argument would astonish rather than convince him !
He would say : 'Can it be so, since we see that men
continually do the one, never the other?' But Butler
insists, and says :—

> That we can do one with greater success than we can the
> other, is no proof that one is less a violation of nature than
> the other. Compassion is a call, a demand of nature, to
> relieve the unhappy, as hunger is a natural call for food.

Surely, *nature*, *natural*, must be used here in a somewhat
artificial manner, in order to get this argument out of
them ! Yet Butler professes to stick to plain facts, not
to sophisticate, not to refine.

> 'Let me take notice,' he says, 'of the danger of going
> beside or beyond the plain, obvious, first appearances of
> things, upon the subject of morals and religion.'

But is it in accordance with the plain, obvious, first
appearances of things, to pronounce compassion to be a
call, a demand of nature to relieve the unhappy, precisely in the same manner as hunger is a natural call for
food ; and to say that to neglect one call is just as much
a violation of nature as the other ? Surely Butler could
not talk in this way, unless he had first laid it down that
all our affections are in themselves equally natural, and
that no degree of greater strength and frequency can
make one affection more natural than the other. They

are all, according to him, voices of God. But the principle
of reflexion or conscience,—a higher voice of God,—
decides how and when each is to be followed. And when
Butler has laid this down, he has no difficulty in affirming that it is as unnatural not to relieve the distressed as
not to eat when one is hungry. Only one feels, not
convinced and satisfied, but in doubt whether he *ought*
to have laid it down, when one sees that it conducts him
to such an affirmation.

Yet once more. The affection of compassion not only
proves that it is as unnatural to turn away from distress
as to turn from food when one is hungry. It proves, also,
that this world was intended neither to be a mere scene
of unhappiness and sorrow, nor to be a state of any
great satisfaction or high enjoyment. And it suggests the
following lesson for us :—

There being that distinct affection implanted in the
nature of man tending to lessen the miseries of life, that provision made for abating its sorrows more than for increasing
its positive happiness, this may suggest to us what should be
our general aim respecting ourselves in our passage through
this world, namely, to endeavour chiefly to escape misery, keep
free from uneasiness, pain, and sorrow, or to get relief and
mitigation of them ; to propose to ourselves peace and tran-
quillity of mind rather than pursue after high enjoyments.

And Butler goes' on to enumerate several so-called

high enjoyments, such as ' to make pleasure and mirth
and jollity our business, to be constantly hurrying about
after some gay amusement, some new gratification of
sense or appetite.' And he points out, what no wise
man will dispute, that these do not confer happiness, and
that we do wrong to make them our end in life. No
doubt ; yet meanwhile, in his main assertion that man's
proper aim is escape from misery rather than positive
happiness, Butler goes clean counter to the most intimate,
the most sure, the most irresistible instinct of human
nature. As a little known but profound French moralist,
Senancour, has said admirably : ' The aim for man is to
augment the feeling of joy, to make our expansive energy
bear fruit, and to combat, in all thinking beings, the
principle of degradation and misery.' But Butler goes
counter, also, to the clear voice of our religion. ' Rejoice and give thanks !' exhorts the Old Testament ;
' Rejoice evermore !' exhorts the New. This, and not
mere escape from misery, getting freedom from uneasiness,
pain, and sorrow, or getting mitigation of them, is what
(to turn Butler's words against himself) 'the consideration of nature marks out as the course we should follow
and the end we should aim at.' And a scheme of human
nature, meant to serve as a rule for human conduct,
cannot, however ingenious, be said to explain things irre-

sistibly according to the strict truth of our mental constitution, when we find it strongly at variance with the facts
of that constitution on a point of capital importance.

Even at past fifty years of age I approach the subject,
so terrible to undergraduates, of Butler's account of self-
love, with a shiver of uneasiness. Yet I will point out
how Butler's own arbitrary definition of self-love, a definition which the cast of his scheme of human nature renders
necessary, creates the difficulties of his assiduous, laboured, and unsatisfying attempt to reconcile self-love
with benevolence. He describes self-love, occasionally,
as 'a general desire of our own happiness.' And he knew
well enough, that the pursuit of our own interest and
happiness, rightly understood, and the obedience to God's
commands, 'must be in every case one and the same thing.'
Nevertheless, Butler's constant notion of the pursuit of our
interest is, that it is the pursuit of our *temporal* good, as he
calls it; the cool consideration of our own temporal
advantage. And he expressly defines his self-love, which
he names 'a private contracted affection,' as 'a regard to
our private good, our private interest.' Private interest
is the favourite expression: 'a cool pursuit of our private
interest.' Now to say, that there is no opposition between
a general desire for our own happiness, and a love of our
neighbour, has nothing puzzling in it. But to define self-

love as a private contracted affection, consisting in a cool deliberate pursuit of our private interest, and then to say, as Butler does, that from self-love, thus defined, love of our neighbour is no more distant than hatred of our neighbour, is to sophisticate things. Butler may make it out by stipulating that self-love shall merely mean pursuing our private interest, and not pursuing it in any particular manner, just as he makes out that not to relieve the distressed is as unnatural to a man as not to eat when he is hungry, by stipulating that all our affections shall be considered equally natural. But he does not convince a serious student by these refinements, does not carry such a student with him, does not help such a student, therefore, a step nearer towards practice. And a moralist's business is to help towards practice.

The truth is, all this elaborate psychology of Butler's, which satisfies us so little,—so little, to use Coleridge's excellent expression, *finds* us,—is unsatisfying because of its radical defectiveness as natural history. What he calls our instincts and principles of action, which are in truth the most obscure, changing, interdependent of phenomena, Butler takes as if they were things as separate, fixed, and palpable as the bodily organs which the dissector has on his table before him. He takes them as if, just as he now finds them, there

they had always been, and there they must always be ;
as if benevolence had always gone on secreting love of
our neighbour, and compassion a desire to relieve misery,
and conscience right verdicts, just as the liver secretes
oile. Butler's error is that of the early chemists, who
imagined things to be elements which were not, but were
capable of being resolved and decomposed much farther.
And a man who is thrown fairly upon himself, and will
have the naked truth, must feel that it is with Butler's
principles and affections as it was with the elements of
the early chemists ;—they are capable of being resolved
and decomposed much farther, and solid ground is not
reached until they are thus decomposed. ' There is this
principle of reflexion or conscience in mankind.'—' True,'
the student may answer; ' but what and whence is it ?
It had a genesis of some kind, and your account of its
genesis is fantastic. What is its natural genesis, and
what the natural genesis of your benevolence, compassion,
resentment, and all the rest of them ? Till I know this,
I do not know where I am in talking about them.'—But
into this vast, dimly lighted, primordial region of the
natural genesis of man's affections and principles, Butler
never enters.

Yet in this laboratory arose those wonderful com-
ᵖ ⁿ ds with which Butler deals, and the source of his

ruling faculty of conscience is to be traced back thither.
There, out of the simple primary instinct, which we may
call the instinct or effort *to live*, grew our affections ; and
out of the experience of those affections, in their result
upon the instinctive effort to live, grew reflexion, practical reason, conscience.    And the all-ruling effort to live
is, in other words, *the desire for happiness* ; that desire
which Butler,—because he identifies it with self-love,. and
defines self-love as the cool pursuit of our private interest, of our temporal good,—is so anxious to treat as
only one motive out of many, and not authoritative.
And this instinct rules because it is *strongest* ; although
Butler is so anxious that no instinct shall rule because
it is strongest.    And our affections of all kinds, too,
according as they serve this deep instinct or thwart it, are
superior in *strength*,—not in present strength, but in
permanent strength ; and have degrees of *worth* according to that superiority.    And benevolence, or a regard to
the good of others, *does* often conflict with the private
contracted affection of self-love, or a regard to our
private interest, with which Butler denies that it conflicts
at all.    But it has the call to contend with it, and the
right to get the better of it, because of its own superiority in *permanent strength*.    And this superiority it
derives from the experience, painfully and slowly ac-

quired, that it serves our instinct to live, our desire
for happiness, better than the private contracted
affection does ; that the private contracted affection, if we follow it, thwarts this instinct. For men
are solidary, or co-partners; and not isolated. And
conscience, in a question of conflict between a regard
to the good of others and a regard to our private good,
is the sense of experience having proved and established,
that, from this reason of men's being really solidary, our
private good ought in a conflict of such kind to give
way ; and that our nature is violated,—that is, our instinct to live is thwarted,—if it does not. That this
sense finds in us a pre-adaptation to it, and a presentiment of its truth, may be inferred from its being a sense
of facts which are a real condition of human progress.
But whatever may be the case as to our pre-adaptation
to it and presentiment of it, the great matter in favour
of the sense is, that the experience reported by it is *true* ;
that the thing *is* so. People may say, they have not got
this sense that their instinct to live is served by loving
their neighbour ;—they may say that they have, in other
words, a dull and uninformed conscience. But that
does not make the experience the less a true thing, the
real experience of the race. Neither does it make the
sense of this experience to be, any the less, genuine

I 2

conscience. And it is genuine conscience, because it apprehends what does really serve our instinct to live, or desire for happiness. And when Shaftesbury supposes the case of a man thinking vice and selfishness to be truly as much for his advantage as virtue and benevolence, and concludes that such a case is without remedy, the answer is : Not at all ; let such a man get conscience, get right experience. And if the man does not, the result is not that he goes on just as well without it ; the result is, that he is lost.

Butler, indeed, was evidently afraid of making the desire of happiness to be that which we must set out with in explaining human nature. And he was afraid of it for this reason : because he was apprehensive of the contracted self-love, and of the contracted judgments, of the individual. But if we say *the instinct to live* instead of *the desire of happiness*,—and the two mean the same thing, and *life* is a better and more exact word to use than *happiness*, and it is, moreover, the Bible-word,— then the difficulty vanishes. For, as man advances in his development, he becomes aware of two lives, one permanent and impersonal, the other transient and bound to our contracted self ; he becomes aware of two selves, one higher and real, the other inferior and apparent ; and that the instinct in him truly to live, the desire for happiness, is served by following the first self and not the second. It is not the case that the two selves do not conflict ; they do conflict. It is not true that the affections and impulses of both alike are, as Butler says, the voice of God ; the self-love of Butler, the 'cool study of our private interest,' is not the voice of God. It is a hasty, erroneous interpretation by us, in our long, tentative, up-struggling development, of the instinct to live, the desire for happiness, which *is* the voice of our authentic nature, the voice of God. And it has to be corrected by experience. Love of our neighbour, Butler's *benevolence*, is the affection by which experience bids us correct it. Many a hard lesson does the experience involve, many a heavy blow. But the satisfaction of our instinct to live, of our desire for happiness, depends on our making and using the experience.

And so true is this history of the two lives in man, the two selves,—both arising out of the instinct to live in us, out of the feeling after happiness, but one correcting and at last dominating the other,—that the psychology of Jesus Christ, which without the least apparatus of system is yet incomparably exacter than Butler's, as well as incomparably more illuminative and fruitful,— this psychology, I say, carries every one with it when it treats these two lives in man, these two selves, as an

evident, capital fact of human nature. Jesus Christ
said : ' Renounce *thyself!* ' and yet he also said : ' What
is a man profited, if he gain the whole world, and yet
lose *himself,* be mulcted of *himself?* ' He said : ' I am
come that men might have *life,* and might have it more
abundantly ; and ye will not come to me that ye may
have *life!* ' And yet he also said : ' Whosoever will save
his *life,* shall lose it.' So certain is it that we have two
lives, two selves ; and that there is no danger in making
the instinct to live, the desire of happiness, to be, as
it really is, that which we must set out with in explaining
human nature, if we add that only in the impersonal
life, and with the higher self, is the instinct truly served
and the desire truly satisfied ; that experience is the
long, painful, irresistible, glorious establishment of this
fact, and that conscience is the recognition of that experience.

Now, as Butler fears to set out, in explaining human
nature, with the desire for happiness, because he imagines
each man cutting and carving arbitrarily for his own
private interest in pursuit of happiness, so he apprehends
a man's cutting and carving arbitrarily, and with mistaken
judgment, for the happiness of others. He supposes a
man fancying that an overbalance of happiness to mankind may be produced by committing some great in-

justice, and says very truly that a man is not on that
account to commit it. And he concludes that 'we are
constituted so as to condemn injustice abstracted from
all consideration what conduct is likeliest to produce an
overbalance of happiness or misery.' And he thinks
that his theory of our affections being all implanted
separately in us, ready-made and full-grown, by a Divine
Author of Nature, his theory of the dignified indepen-
dence, on the part of virtue and conscience, of all aim
at happiness, is thereby proved. So far from it, that man
did not even propose to himself the worthier aim, as it
now is seen by us to be, of the production of *general*
happiness, in feeling his way to the laws of virtue.
He proposed to himself the production simply of his
own happiness. But experience of what made for *this*,
such experience slowly led him to the laws of virtue ;—
laws abridging in a hundred ways what at first seemed
his own happiness, and implying the solidarity of himself and his happiness with the race and theirs. This is
what experience brought him to, and what conscience is
concerned with : a number of laws determining our conduct in many ways, and implying our solidarity with others.
But experience did not bring him to the rule of every
man just aiming, 'according to the best of his judgment,'
at what might 'have the appearance of being likely to

produce an overbalance of happiness to mankind in their present state.' It did not conduct him to this, or establish for him any such rule of action as this. This is not his *experience*, and conscience turns on experience. It is not in the form of carving for men's apparent happiness in defiance of the common rules of justice and virtue, that the duty of caring for other men's happiness makes itself felt to us, but in the form of an obedience to the common rules themselves of justice and of virtue. Those rules, however, had indubitably in great part their rise in the experience, that, by seeking solely his own private happiness, a man made shipwreck of life.

In morals, we must not rely just on what may 'have the appearance' to the individual, but on the experience of the race as to happiness. To that experience, the individual, as one of the race, is profoundly and intimately adapted. He may much more safely conform himself to such experience than to his own crude judgments upon 'appearances;' nay, such experience has, if he deals with himself fairly, a much stronger hold upon his conviction. Butler confuses the foreseen overbalance of happiness or misery, which, as the result of experience in the race, has silently and slowly determined our calling actions virtuous or vicious, with that overbalance which each transient individual may think

he can foresee. The transient individual must not cut
and carve in the results of human experience, according to his crude notions of what may constitute human
happiness. His thought of the obligation laid upon
him by those rules of justice and virtue, wherein the
moral experience of our race has been summed up,
must rather be : 'The will of mortal man did not beget
it, neither shall oblivion ever put it to sleep.' But the
rules had their origin in man's desire for happiness notwithstanding.

2.

Impressive, then, as the *Sermons at the Rolls* are, and
much as they contain which is precious, I do not think
that these sermons, setting forth Butler's theory of the
foundation of morals, will satisfy any one who in dis-
quietude, and seeking earnestly for a sure stay, comes
for help to them. But the *Sermons at the Rolls* were
published in 1726, when Butler was but thirty-four years
old. They were all preached in the eight years between 1718 and 1726,—between the twenty-sixth year of
Butler's life and the thirty-fourth. The date is important. At that age a man is, I think, more likely to
attempt a highly systematic, intricate theory of human
nature and morals, than he is afterwards. And if he

does attempt it, it cannot well be satisfactory. The man
is hardly ripe for it, he has not had enough experience.
So at least, one is disposed to say, as one regards the
thing from the point of view of a more mature age oneself. The *Analogy* did not come till ten years after the
Sermons. The *Analogy* appeared in 1736, when Butler
was forty-four. It is a riper work than the *Sermons at
the Rolls*. Perhaps it will seem in me the very height
of over-partiality to the merits of old age, of that un-
popular condition which I am myself approaching, if I
say, that I would rather have had the *opus magnum* of
such a man as Butler, and on such a subject as the
philosophy of religion, ten years later from him still. I
would rather have had it from him at fifty-four than at
forty-four. To me, the most entirely satisfactory productions of Butler are the *Six Sermons on Public
Occasions*, all of them later than the *Analogy* ; the
*Charge to the Clergy of Durham*, delivered the year
before his death ; and a few fragments, also dating
from the close of his life.

But let us be thankful for what we have. The *Analogy* is a work of great power ; to read it, is a very valuable mental exercise. Not only does it contain, like the
Sermons, many trains of thought and many single obser-
vations which are profound and precious, but the intel-

lectual conduct of the work, so to speak, seems to me
to be more that of a master, to be much firmer and
clearer, more free from embarrassment and confusion,
than that of the Sermons. Of course the form of the
work gave Butler advantages which with the form of a
sermon he could not have. But the mental grasp, too,
is, I think, visibly stronger in the *Analogy*.

I have drawn your attention to the terms of unbounded praise in which the *Analogy* is extolled. It is
called ' unanswerable.' It is said to be ' the most original and profound work extant in any language on the
philosophy of religion.' It is asserted, that, by his
*Analogy*, Butler ' placed metaphysic, which till then had
nothing to support it but mere abstraction or shadowy
speculation, on the firm basis of observation and experiment.'

I have also told you what is to my mind the one sole
point of interest for us now, in a work like the *Analogy*.
To those who search earnestly,—amid that break-up of
traditional and conventional notions respecting our life,
its conduct, and its sanctions, which is undeniably be-
falling our age,—for some clear light and some sure stay,
does the *Analogy* afford it to them ? A religious work
cannot touch us very deeply as a mere intellectual feat.
Whether the *Analogy* was or was not calculated to

make the loose Deists of fashionable circles, in the year
of grace 1736, feel uncomfortable, we do not, as I said
the other night, care two straws, unless we hold the
argumentative positions of those Deists ; and we do not.
What has the *Analogy* got to enlighten and help *us ?* is
the one important question.

Its object is to make men embrace religion. And
that is just what we all ought most to desire : to make
men embrace religion, which we may see to be full of
what is salutary for them. Yet how many of them will
not embrace it ! Now, to every one with whom the im-
pediment to its reception is not simply moral,—culpable
levity, or else a secret leaning to vice,—Butler professes
to make out clearly in his *Analogy* that they *ought* to
embrace it, and to embrace it, moreover, in the form of
what is called orthodox Christianity, with its theosophy
and miracles. And he professes to establish this by the
analogy of religion,—first of natural religion, then of revealed religion,—to the constitution and laws of nature.

Elsewhere I have remarked what advantage Butler
had against the Deists of his own time, in the line of
argument which he chose. But how does his argument
in itself stand the scrutiny of one who has no counter-
thesis, such as that of the Deists, to make good against
Butler ? How does it affect one who has no wish at all

to doubt or cavil, like the loose wits of fashionable society who angered Butler, still less any wish to mock ; but who comes to the *Analogy* with an honest desire to receive from it anything which he finds he can use ?

Now, I do not remember to have anywhere seen pointed out the precise break-down, which such an inquirer must, it seems to me, be conscious of in Butler's argument from analogy. The argument is of this kind :— The reality of the laws of moral government of *this* world, says Butler, implies, by analogy, a like reality of laws of moral government in the second world, where we shall be hereafter.—The analogy is, in truth, used to prove not only the probable continuance of the laws of moral government, but also the probable existence of that future world in which they will be manifested. It *does* only prove the probable continuance of the laws of moral government in the future world, *supposing* that second world to exist. But for that existence it supplies no probability whatever. For it is not the laws of moral government which give us proof of this present world in which they are manifested ; it is the experience that this present world actually exists, and is a place in which these laws are manifested. Show us, we may say to Butler, that a like place presents itself over again after we are dead, and we will allow that by analogy the same moral laws will probably continue to govern it.    But this is all which analogy can prove in the matter.    The positive existence of the world to come must be proved, like the positive existence of the present world, by *experience*.   And of this experience Butler's argument furnishes, and can furnish, not one tittle.

There may be other reasons for believing in a second life beyond the grave.   Christians in general consider that they get such grounds from revelation.   And people who come to Butler with the belief already established, are not likely to ask themselves very closely what Butler's analogical reasoning on its behalf is good for.   The reasoning is exercised in support of a thesis which does not require to be made out for them.   But whoever comes to Butler in a state of. genuine uncertainty, and has to lean with his whole weight on Butler's reasonings for support, will soon discover their fundamental weakness.    The weakness goes through the *Analogy* from beginning to end.   For example :—

The states of life in which we ourselves existed formerly, in the womb and in our infancy, are almost as different from our present in mature age as it is possible to conceive any two states or degrees of life can be.   Therefore, that we are to exist hereafter in a state as different (suppose) from our present as this is from the former, is but according to the analogy of nature.

There it is in the first chapter! But we have *experience* of the several different states succeeding one another in man's present life ; that is what makes us believe in their succeeding one another here. We have no experience of a further different state beyond the limits of this life. If we had, we might freely admit that analogy renders it probable that that state may be as unlike to our actual state, as our actual state is to our state in the womb or in infancy. But that there *is* the further different state must first, for the argument from analogy to take effect, be proved from experience.

Again :—

' Sleep, or, however, a swoon, shows us,' says Butler, ' that our living powers exist when they are not exercised, and when there is no present capacity for exercising them. Therefore, there can no probability be collected from the reason of the thing that death will be their destruction.'

But ' the reason of the thing,' in this matter, is simply experience ; and we have experience of the living powers existing on through a swoon, we have none of their existing on through death.

Or, again, the form of the argument being altered, but its vice being still of just the same character :—' All presumption of death's being the destruction of living beings must go upon supposition that they are compounded and so discerptible.' So says Butler, and then off he goes upon a metaphysical argument about consciousness being a single and indivisible power. But a doubter, who is dealing quite simply with himself, will stop Butler before ever his metaphysical argument begins, and say: 'Not at all ; the presumption of death's being the destruction of living beings does not go upon the supposition that they are compounded and so discerptible ; it goes upon the unbroken experience that the living powers then cease.'

Once more. 'We see by experience,' says Butler, 'that men may lose their limbs, their organs of sense, and even the greatest part of their bodies, and yet remain the same living agents.' Yes, we do. But that conscious life is possible with *some* of our bodily organs gone, does not prove that it is possible without *any*. We admit the first because it is shown to us by experience ; we have no experience of the second.

I say, a man who is looking seriously for firm ground, cannot but soon come to perceive what Butler's argument in the *Analogy* really amounts to, and that there is no help to be got from it. 'There is no shadow of anything unreasonable,' begins Butler always, 'in conceiving so-and-so,—in the conception of natural religion, in the conception of revealed religion.' The answer of any earnest man must be in some words of Butler's own : 'Suppositions are not to be looked on as true, because not incredible.' ' But,' says Butler, ' it is a fact that this life exists, and there are analogies in this life to the supposed system of natural and revealed religion. The existence of that system, therefore, is a fact also.' ' Nay,' is the answer, 'but we affirm the fact of this life, not because " there is no shadow of anything unreasonable in conceiving it," but because we experience it.' As to the *fact*, experience is the touchstone.

' There is nothing incredible,' argues Butler again, ' that God, the moral and intelligent Author of all things, will reward and punish men for their actions hereafter, for the whole course of nature is a present instance of his exercising that government over us which implies in it rewarding and punishing.' But how far does our positive experience go in this matter? What is fact of positive experience is, that inward satisfaction (let us fully concede this to Butler) follows one sort of actions, and inward dissatisfaction another ; and, moreover, that also outward rewards and punishments do very gene- rally follow certain actions. In this sense we *are* pu nished and rewarded ; that is certain. And one must add, surely, that our not being punished and rewarded more completely and regularly might quite well, one

would think, have been what suggested to mankind the
notion of a second life, with a restitution of all things.
But, be that as it may, we have no *experience*,—I say
what is the mere undoubted fact,—we have no *experience* that it is a quasi-human agent, whom Butler calls
the Author of Nature, a Being moral and intelligent, who
thus rewards and punishes us.

But Butler alleges, that we have, not indeed experience of this, but demonstration.   For he says that a
uniform course of operation, this world as we see it, *nature*,
necessarily implies an operating agent.   It necessarily
implies an intelligent designer with a will and a character,
a ruler all-wise and all-powerful.   And this quasi-human
agent, this intelligent designer with a will and a character,
since he is all-wise and all-powerful, and since he governs
the world, and evidently, by what we see of natural rewards
and punishments, exercises moral government over us here,
but admittedly not more than in *some degree*, not yet *the
perfection* of moral government,—this Governor must
be reserving the complete consummation of his moral
government for a second world hereafter.   And the
strength of Butler's argument against the Deists lay here:
that they held, as he did, that a quasi-human agent, an
intelligent designer with a will and a character, was demonstrably the author and governor of nature.

But in this supposed demonstrably true starting-point,

common both to Butler and to the Deists, we are in full
metaphysics. We are in that world of ' mere abstraction
or shadowy speculation,' from which Butler was said to
have rescued us and placed us on the firm basis of observation and experiment. The proposition that this
world, as we see it, necessarily implies an intelligent designer with a will and a character, a quasi-human agent
and governor, cannot, I think, but be felt, by any one
who is brought fairly face to face with it and has to rest
everything upon it, not to be self-demonstrating, nay, to
be utterly impalpable. Evidently it is not of the same
experimental character as the proposition that we *are*
rewarded and punished according to our actions ; or
that, as St. Augustine says : *Sibi pœna est omnis in-
ordinatus animus.* The proposition of St. Augustine
produces, when it is urged, a sense of satisfying conviction, and we can go on to build upon it. But will
any one say that the proposition, that the course of
nature implies an operating agent with a will and a character, produces or can produce a like sense of satisfying
conviction, and can in like manner be built upon? It
cannot. It does not appeal, like the other, to what is
solid. It appeals, really, to the deep anthropomorphic
tendency in man ; and this tendency, when we examine
the thing coolly, we feel that we cannot trust.

K 2

However, the proposition is thought to have scientific support in arguments drawn from *being, essence.* But even thus supported it never, I think, can produce in any one a sense of satisfying conviction ; it produces, at most, a sense of puzzled submission.  To build religion, or anything else which is to stand firm, upon such a sense as this, is vain.  Religion must be built on ideas about which there is no puzzle.  Therefore, in order to get rid of this foundation of puzzle for religion, and with a view to substituting a surer foundation, I have elsewhere tried to show in what confusion the metaphysical arguments drawn from *being, essence,* for an intelligent author of nature with a will and a character, have their rise.  The assertion of such an author is then left with our anthropomorphic instinct as its sole warrant, and is seen not to be a safe foundation whereon to build all our certainties in religion.   It is not axiomatic, it is not experimental. It deals with what is, in my judgment, altogether beyond our experience ; it is purely abstract and speculative.   A plain man, when he is asked how he can affirm that a house is made by an intelligent designer with a will and a character, and yet doubt whether a tree is made by an intelligent designer with a will and a character, must surely answer that he affirms a house to have been made by such a designer because he has experience of the fact, but that of the fact of a tree being made by such a designer he has none. And if pressed, how then can the tree possibly be there ? surely the answer : ' Perhaps from the tendency to grow ! ' is not so very unreasonable.

Butler admits that the assertion of his all-foreseeing, all-powerful designer, with a will and a character, involves grave difficulties. ' Why anything of hazard and danger should be put upon such frail creatures as we are, may well be thought a difficulty in speculation.' But he appeals, and no man ever appealed more impressively than he, to the sense we must have of our ignorance. Difficulties of this kind, he says, ' are so apparently and wholly founded in our ignorance, that it is wonderful they should be insisted upon by any but such as are weak enough to think they are acquainted with the whole system of things.' And he speaks of ' that infinitely absurd supposition that we know the whole of the case.' But does not the common account of God by theologians, does not Butler's own assertion of the all-foreseeing, quasi-human designer, with a will and a character, go upon the supposition that we know, at any rate, a very great deal, and more than we actually do know, of the case ? And are not the difficulties alleged created by that supposition ? And is not the appeal to

our ignorance in fact an appeal to us, having taken a
great deal for granted, to take something more for
granted :—namely, that what we at first took for granted
has a satisfactory solution somewhere beyond the reach
of our knowledge?

Then, however, the argument from analogy is again
used to solve our difficulties. It is hard to understand
how an almighty moral Creator and Governor, designing
the world as a place of moral discipline for man, should
have so contrived things that the moral discipline altogether
fails, in a vast number of cases, to take effect. Butler,
however, urges, that the world may have been intended
by its infinite almighty Author and Governor for moral
discipline, although, even, 'the generality of men do not
improve or grow better in it ;' because we see that 'of
the seeds of vegetables, and bodies of animals, far the
greatest part decay before they are improved to maturity,
and appear to be utterly destroyed.' But surely the
natural answer is, that there is no difficulty about millions
of seeds missing their perfection, because we do not
suppose nature an Infinite Almighty and Moral Being ;
but that the difficulty in the other case is because we do
suppose God such a Being.

However, against the Deists who started with as-
suming a quasi-human agent, a Being of infinite wisdom

and power with a will and a character, as a necessary
conception, Butler's argument is very effective. And he
says expressly that in his *Analogy* the validity of this
conception 'is a principle gone upon as proved, and
generally known and confessed to be proved.' But,
however, Butler in his *Analogy* affirms also (and the
thing is important to be noted) 'the direct and fundamental proof of Christianity' to be, just what the mass of
its adherents have always supposed it to be :—miracles
and the fulfilment of prophecy. And from a man like
Butler this dictum will certainly require attention, even
on the part of an inquirer who feels that Butler's metaphysics, and his argument from analogy, are unavailing.

But any clear-sighted inquirer will soon perceive that
Butler's ability for handling these important matters of
miracles and prophecy is not in proportion to his great
powers of mind, and to his vigorous and effective use of
those powers on other topics. Butler could not well,
indeed, have then handled miracles and prophecy satisfactorily ; the time was not ripe for it. Men's knowledge
increases, their point of view changes, they come to
see things differently. That is the reason, without any
pretence of intellectual superiority, why men are now
able to view miracles and prophecy more justly than
Butler did. The insufficiency of his treatment of them is,

indeed, manifest. Can anything be more express or determinate, he asks, than the fulfilment of prophecy mentioned in the Epistle to the Hebrews,—the fulfilment of
the words, ' Sacrifice and offering thou wouldest not,
but a *body* hast thou prepared me,' by the offering for
man's sins of the *body* of Jesus Christ upon the cross?
A man like Butler could not nowadays use an argument
like that. He could not be unaware that the writer of
the Epistle is using the false rendering of the Greek
Bible, *a body hast thou prepared me*, instead of the true
rendering of the original, *mine ears hast thou opened*, and
gets his fulfilment of prophecy out of that false rendering ;—a fulfilment, therefore, which is none at all.

Neither could Butler now speak of the Bible-history
being all of it equally 'authentic genuine history,' or
argue in behalf of this thesis as he does. It must evidently all stand or fall together, he argues ; now, 'there
are characters in the Bible with all the internal marks
imaginable of their being real.' Most true, is the answer ;
there is plenty of fact in the Bible, there is also plenty of
legend. John the Baptist and Simon Peter have all the
internal marks imaginable of their being real characters ;
granted. But one Gospel makes Jesus disappear into
Egypt directly after his birth, another makes him stay
quietly on in Palestine. That John the Baptist and

Simon Peter are real characters does not make this consistent history. As well say that because Mirabeau and Danton are real characters, an addition to Louis the Sixteenth's history which made him to be spirited away from Varennes into Germany, and then to come back after some time and resume his career in France, would not jar. No. 'Things are what they are, and the consequences of them will be what they will be.' And the accounts in the Gospels of the Holy Child's incarnation and infancy, and very many things in the Bible besides, are legends.

Again. 'The belief of miracles by the Apostles and their contemporaries must be a proof of those facts, for they were such as came under the observation of their senses.' The simple answer is : 'But we know what the observation of men's senses, under certain circumstances, is worth.' Yet further : 'Though it is not of equal weight, yet it is of weight, that the martyrs of the next age, notwithstanding they were not eye-witnesses of those facts, as were the Apostles and their contemporaries, had however full opportunity to inform themselves whether they were true or not, and gave equal proof of their believing them to be true.' The simple answer again is : 'The martyrs never dreamed of informing themselves about the miracles in the manner supposed; for they never dreamed of doubting them, and could not have dreamed of it.' If Butler cannot prove religion and Christianity by his reasonings from metaphysics and from analogy, most certainly he will not prove them by these reasonings on Bible-history.

But the wonderful thing about the *Analogy* is the poor insignificant result, even in Butler's own judgment,— the puny total outcome,—of all this accumulated evidence from analogy, metaphysics, and Bible-history. It is, after all, only ' evidence which keeps the mind in doubt, perhaps in perplexity.' The utmost it is calculated to beget is, ' a serious doubting apprehension that it *may* be true.' However, ' in the daily course of life,' says Butler, ' our nature and condition necessarily require us to act upon evidence much lower than what is commonly called probable.' In a matter, then, of such immense practical importance as religion, where the bad consequences of a mistake may be so incalculable, we ought, he says, un-hesitatingly to act upon imperfect evidence. ' It ought, in all reason, considering its infinite importance, to have nearly the same influence upon practice, as if it were thoroughly believed !' And such is, really, the upshot of the *Analogy*. Such is, when all is done, the ' happy alliance' achieved by it ' between faith and philosophy.'

But we *do* not, in the daily course of life, act upon

evidence which *we ourselves conceive* to be much lower than what is commonly called probable. If I am going to take a walk out of Edinburgh, and thought of choosing the Portobello road, and a travelling menagerie is taking the same road, it is certainly possible that a tiger may escape from the menagerie and devour me if I take that road ; but the evidence that he will is certainly, also, much lower than what is commonly called probable. Well, I do not, on that low degree of evidence, avoid the Porto-bello road and take another. But the duty of acting on such a sort of evidence is really made by Butler the motive for a man's following the road of religion,—the way of peace.

How unlike, above all, is this motive to the motive always supposed in the book itself of our religion, in the Bible ! After reading the *Analogy* one goes instinctively to bathe one's spirit in the Bible again, to be refreshed by its boundless certitude and exhilaration. ' The Eternal is the strength of my life !' 'The foundation of God standeth sure'!—that is the constant tone of religion in the Bible. ' If I tell you the *truth,* why do ye not believe me?—the *evident* truth, that whoever comes to me has life ; and evident, because whoever *does* come, gets it !' That is the evidence to constrain our practice which is offered by Christianity.

3.

Let us, then, confess it to ourselves plainly. The *Analogy*, the great work on which such immense praise has been lavished, is, for all real intents and purposes now, a failure ; it does not serve. It seemed once to have a spell and a power ; but the *Zeit-Geist* breathes upon it, and we rub our eyes, and it has the spell and the power no longer. It has the effect upon me, as I contemplate it, of a stately and severe fortress, with thick and high walls, built of old to control the kingdom of evil ;—but the gates are open, and the guards gone.

For to control the kingdom of evil the work was, no doubt, designed. Whatever may be the proper tendencies of Deism as a speculative opinion, there can be no doubt, I think, that the loose Deism of fashionable circles, as seen by Butler, had a tendency to minimise religion and morality, to reduce and impair their authority. Butler's Deists were, in fact, for the most part free-living people who said, *We are Deists*, as the least they could say ; as another mode of saying : ' We think little of religion in general, and of Christianity in particular.' Butler, who felt to the bottom of his soul the obligation of religion in general, and of Christianity in particular, set himself to establish the obligation of them against these

lax people, who in fact denied it. And the religion and
the Christianity, of which Butler set himself to establish
the obligation, were religion and Christianity in the form
then received and current. And in this form he could
establish their obligation as against his Deistical opponents. But he could not establish them so as quite to
suit his own mind and soul, so as to satisfy himself fully.

Hence his labour and sorrow, his air of weariness,
depression, and gloom ;—the air of a man who cannot
get beyond 'evidence which keeps the mind in doubt,
perhaps in perplexity.' Butler 'most readily acknow-
ledges that the foregoing treatise' (his *Analogy*) ' is by no
means satisfactory ; very far indeed from it.' He quotes
the Preacher's account of what he himself had found in
life, as the true account of what man may expect here
below :—' Great ignorance of the works of God and the
method of his providence in the government of the world;
great labour and weariness in the search and observation he employs himself about ; and great disappoint-
ment, pain, and even vexation of mind upon that which
he remarks of the appearances of things and of what is
going forward upon this earth.' 'The result of the
Preacher's whole review and inspection is,' says Butler,
' sorrow, perplexity, a sense of his necessary ignorance.'
That is certainly a true description of the impression the

Preacher leaves on us of his own frame of mind ; and
it is not a bad description of Butler's frame of mind also.
But so far is it from being a true description of the right
tone and temper of man according to the Bible-conception
of it, that the Book of Ecclesiastes, which seems to re-
commend that temper, was nearly excluded from the
Canon on this very account, and was only saved by its
animating return, in its last verses, to the genuine tradition
of Israel : ' Let us hear the conclusion of the whole
matter: fear God and keep his commandments, for that
is the whole duty of man.'

But yet, in spite of his gloom, in spite of the failure
of his *Analogy* to serve our needs, Butler remains a
personage of real grandeur for us.   This pathetic figure,
with its earnestness, its strenuous rectitude, its firm faith
both in religion and in reason, does in some measure
help us, does point the way for us.   Butler's profound
sense, that inattention to religion implies 'a dissolute immoral temper of mind,' engraves itself upon his readers'
thoughts also, and comes to govern them.   His conviction, that religion and Christianity do somehow ' in themselves entirely fall in with our natural sense of things,' that
they are true, and that their truth, moreover, is somehow
to be established and justified on plain grounds of reason,
—this wholesome and invaluable conviction, also, gains

us as we read him. The ordinary religionists of Butler's day might well be startled, as they were, by this bishop with the strange, novel, and unhallowed notion, full of dangerous consequence, of 'referring mankind to a law of nature or virtue, written on their hearts.' The pamphleteer, who accused Butler of dying a Papist, declares plainly that he for his part 'has no better opinion of the certainty, clearness, uniformity, universality, &c., of this law, than he has of the importance of external religion.' But Butler *did* believe in the certainty of this law. It was the real foundation of things for him. With awful reverence, he saluted, and he set himself to study and to follow, this 'course of life marked out for man by nature, whatever that nature be.' And he was for perfect fairness of mind in considering the evidence for this law, or for anything else. 'It is fit things be stated and considered as they really are.' 'Things are what they are, and the consequences of them will be what they will be; why, then, should we desire to be deceived?' And he believed in reason. 'I express myself with caution, lest I should be mistaken to vilify reason, which is indeed the only faculty we have wherewith to judge concerning anything, even religion itself.' Such was Butler's fidelity to that sacred light to which religion makes too many people false,—reason.

It always seems to me, that with Butler's deep sense
that 'the government of the world is carried on by
general laws ;' with his deep sense, too, of our ignorance,—
nay, that ' it is indeed, in general, no more than effects
that the most knowing are acquainted with, for as to
*causes,* they are as entirely in the dark as the most ignorant,'—he would have found no insuperable difficulty
in bringing himself to regard the power of ' the law of
virtue we are born under,' as an idea equivalent to the
religious idea of the power of God, without determining,
or thinking that he had the means to determine, whether
this power was a quasi-human agent or not.   But a
second world under a righteous judge, who should redress
the imperfect balance of things as they are in this world,
seemed to Butler indispensable.   Yet no one has spoken
more truly and nobly than he, of the natural victoriousness
of virtue, even in this world.   He finds a tendency of
virtue to prevail, which he can only describe as ' somewhat moral in the essential constitution of things ;' as ' a
declaration from the Author of Nature, determinate and
not to be evaded, in favour of virtue and against vice.'
True, virtue is often overborne.   But this is plainly a
perversion.   ' Our finding virtue to be hindered from
procuring to itself its due superiority and advantages, is
no objection against its having, in the essential nature of

the thing, a tendency to procure them.' And he can see, he says, 'in the nature of things, a tendency in virtue and vice to produce the good and bad effects now mentioned, in a greater degree than they do in fact produce them.' Length of time, however, is required for working this fully out ; whereas 'men are impatient and for precipitating things.' ' There must be sufficient length of time ; the complete success of virtue, as of reason, cannot, from the nature of the thing, be otherwise than gradual.' 'Still, the constitution of our nature is as it is ; our happiness and misery *are* trusted to our conduct, and made to depend upon it.' And our comfort of hope is, that 'though the higher degree of distributive justice, which nature points out and leads towards, is prevented for a time from taking place, it is by obstacles which the state of this world unhappily throws in its way, and which are in their nature temporary.' And Butler supposes and describes an ideal society upon earth, where 'this happy tendency of virtue,' as he calls it, should at last come to prevail, in a way which brings straight to our thoughts and to our lips the Bible-expression : *the kingdom of God.* However, Butler decides that good men cannot now unite sufficiently to bring this better society about ; that it cannot, therefore, be brought about in the present known

L

course of nature, and that it must be meant to come to pass in another world beyond the grave.

Now, the very expression which I have just used, *the kingdom of God*, does certainly, however little it may at present be usual with religious people to think so, it does certainly suggest a different conclusion from Butler's. It does point to a transformation of this present world through the victory of what Butler calls virtue, and what the Bible calls righteousness, and what in general religious people call goodness ; it does suggest such transformation as possible. This transformation is the great original idea of the Christian Gospel ; nay, it is properly the Gospel or *good news* itself. 'The kingdom of God is at hand,' said Jesus Christ, when he first came preaching ; ' repent, and believe the good news.' Jesus ' talked ' to the people 'about the kingdom of God.' He told the young man, whom he called to follow him, to 'go and spread the news of the kingdom of God.' In the Acts, we find the disciples 'preaching the kingdom of God,' 'testifying concerning the kingdom of God,' still in their Master's manner and words. And it is undeniable that whoever thinks that virtue and goodness will finally come to prevail in this present world so as to transform it, who believes that they are even now surely though slowly prevailing, and himself does all he can to help the work

forward,—as he acquires in this way an experimental
sense of the truth of Christianity which is of the
strongest possible kind, so he is, also, entirely in the tradition and ideas of the Founder of Christianity. In
like manner, whoever places immortal life in coming to
live, even here in this present world, with that higher
and impersonal life on which, in speaking of self-love,
we insisted,—and in thus no longer living to himself but
*living*, as St. Paul says, *to God*,—does entirely conform
himself to the doctrine and example of the Saviour of
mankind, Jesus Christ, who ' annulled death, and brought
life and immortality to light through the Gospel.' And
could Butler, whose work has many precious and instructive pointings this way, have boldly entered the way
and steadily pursued it, his work would not, I think,
have borne the embarrassed, inconclusive, and even
mournful character, which is apparent in it now.

Let us not, however, overrate the mournfulness of
this great man, or underrate his consolations. The power
of religion which actuated him was, as is the case with so
many of us, better, profounder, and happier, than the
scheme of religion which he could draw out in his books.
Nowhere does this power show itself more touchingly
than in a fragment or two,—memoranda for his own use,—
which are among the last things that his pen wrote

before death brushed it from his hand for ever. 'Hunger and thirst after righteousness,' he writes, 'till filled with it by being made partaker of the divine nature !' And again he writes, using and underscoring words of the Latin Vulgate which are more earnest and expressive than the words of our English version in that place : ' *Sicut oculi servorum* intenti sunt *ad manum dominorum suorum, sicut oculi ancillæ ad manum dominæ suæ, ita oculi nostri ad Deum nostrum, donec misereatur nostri;—* As the eyes of servants *are bent* towards the hand of their masters, and the eyes of a maiden towards the hand of her mistress, even so are our eyes towards our God, until he have mercy upon us.'

Let us leave Butler, after all our long scrutiny of him, with these for his last words !

## *THE CHURCH OF ENGLAND.*[1]

I HAVE heard it confidently asserted, that the Church of England is an institution so thoroughly artificial, and of which the justification, if any justification for it can be found, must be sought in reasons so extremely far-fetched, that only highly trained and educated people can be made to see that it has a possible defence at all, and that to undertake its defence before a plain audience of working men would be hopeless. It would be very interesting to try the experiment ; and I had long had a half-formed design of endeavouring to show to an audience of working men the case, as I for my part conceived it, on behalf of the Church of England. But meanwhile there comes to me my friend, your President, and reminds me of an old request of his that I should some day speak in this hall, and presses me to comply with it this very season. And if I am to speak at Sion College, and to the London clergy, and at this juncture,

[1] The following discourse was delivered as an address to the London clergy at Sion College.

how can I help remembering my old design of speaking
about the Church of England ;—remembering it, and
being tempted, though before a very different audience,
to take that subject?

Jeremy Taylor says : ' Every minister ought to concern himself in the faults of them that are present, but
not of the absent.'   ' Every minister,' he says again,
' ought to preach to his hearers and urge *their* duty ; St.
John the Baptist told the soldiers what the soldiers should
do, but troubled not their heads with what was the duty
of the Scribes and Pharisees.'   And certainly one should
not defend the Church of England to an audience of
clergy and to an audience of artisans in quite the same
way.   But perhaps one ought not to care to put at all
before the clergy the case for the Church of England,
but rather one should bring before them the case against
it.   For the case of the Church of England is supposed
to be their own case, and they are the parties interested ;
and to commend their own case to the parties interested
is useless, but what may do them most good is rather to
show them its defects.   And in this view, the profitable
thing for the London clergy at Sion College to hear,
would be, perhaps, a lecture on disestablishment, an
exhortation to ' happy despatch.'

Yet this is not so, for the simple reason that the Church

of England is not a private sect but a national institution. There can be no greater mistake than to regard the cause of the Church of England as the cause of the clergy, and the clergy as the parties concerned for the maintenance of the Church of England. The clergy are a very small minority of the nation. As the Church of England will not be abolished to gratify the jealousy of this and that private sect, also a small minority of the nation, so neither will it be maintained to gratify the interest of the clergy. Public institutions must have public reasons for existing ; and if at any time there arise circumstances and dangers which induce a return to those reasons, so as to set them in a clear light to oneself again and to make sure of them, the clergy may with just as much propriety do this, or assist at its being done,—nay, they are as much bound to do it,—as any other members of the community.

But some one will perhaps be disposed to say, that though there is no impropriety in your hearing the Church of England defended, yet there is an impropriety in my defending it to you. A man who has published a good deal which is at variance with the body of theological doctrine commonly received in the Church of England and commonly preached by its ministers, cannot well, it may be thought, stand up before the clergy as a friend to their cause and to that of the Church. Pro-

fessed ardent enemies of the Church have assured me
that I am really, in their opinion, one of the worst enemies
that the Church has,—a much worse enemy than themselves.   Perhaps that opinion is shared by some of those
who now hear me.   I make bold to say that it is totally
erroneous.   It is founded in an entire misconception of
the character and scope of what I have written concerning religion.   I regard the Church of England as, in
fact, a great national society for the promotion of what
is commonly called *goodness*, and for promoting it through
the most effectual means possible, the only means which
are really and truly effectual for the object : through the
means of the Christian religion and of the Bible.   This
plain practical object is undeniably the object of the
Church of England and of the clergy.   'Our province,'
says Butler, whose sayings come the more readily to my
mind because I have been very busy with him lately,
' our province is virtue and religion, life and manners,
the science of improving the temper and making the
heart better.   This is the field assigned us to cultivate ;
how much it has lain neglected is indeed astonishing.
He who should find out one rule to assist us in this
work would deserve infinitely better of mankind than all
the improvers of other knowledge put together.'   This is
indeed true religion, true Christianity.   *Illi sunt veri*

*fideles Tui,* says the ' Imitation,' *qui totam vitam suam ad emendationem disponunt.* Undoubtedly this is so ; and the more we come to see and feel it to be so, the more shall we get a happy sense of clearness and certainty in religion.

Now, to put a new construction upon many things that are said in the Bible, to point out errors in the Bible, errors in the dealings of theologians with it, is exactly the sort of ' other knowledge ' which Butler disparages by comparison with a knowledge more important. Perhaps he goes too far when he disparages it so absolutely as in another place he does, where he makes Moses conclude, and appears to agree with Moses in concluding, that ' *the only knowledge,* which is of any avail to us, is that which teaches us our duty, or assists us in the discharge of it.' ' If,' says he, ' the discoveries of men of deep research and curious inquiry serve the cause of virtue and religion, in the way of proof, motive to practice, or assistance in it ; or if they tend to render life less un- happy and promote its satisfactions, then they are most usefully employed; but bringing things to light, alone and of itself, is of no manner of use any otherwise than as entertainment and diversion.' ' Bringing things to light' is not properly to be spoken of, I think, quite in this fashion. Still, with the low *comparative* rank which

Butler assigns to it we will not quarrel. And when Butler urges that 'knowledge is not our proper happiness,' and that 'men of research and curious inquiry should just be put in mind not to mistake what they are doing,' we may all of us readily admit that his admonitions are wise and salutary.

And therefore the object of the Church, which is in large the promotion of goodness, and the business of the clergy, which is to teach men their duty and to assist them in the discharge of it, do really and truly interest me more, and do appear in my eyes as things more valuable and important, than the object and business pursued in those writings of mine which are in question,—writings which seek to put a new construction on much in the Bible, to alter the current criticism of it, to invalidate the conclusions of theologians from it. If the two are to conflict, I had rather that it should be the object and business of those writings which should have to give way. Most certainly the establishment of an improved biblical criticism, or the demolition of the systems of theologians, will never in itself avail to teach men their duty or to assist them in the discharge of it. Perhaps, even, no one can very much give himself to such objects without running some risk of over-valuing their importance and of being diverted by them from practice.

But there are times when practice itself, when the very object of the Church and of the clergy,—the promotion of goodness through the instrumentality of the Christian religion and of the Bible,—is endangered, with many persons, from the predominance of the systems of theologians, and from the want of a new and better construction than theirs to put upon the Bible. And ours is a time of this kind; such, at least, is my conviction. Nor are persons free to say that we had better all of us stick to practice, and resolve not to trouble ourselves with speculative questions of biblical and theological criticism. No; such questions catch men in a season and manner which does not depend on their own will, and often their whole spirit is bewildered by them and their former hold on practice seems threatened. Well then, at this point and for those persons, the criticism which I have attempted is designed to come in; when, for want of some such new criticism, their practical hold on the Bible and on the Christian religion seems to be threatened. The criticism is not presented as something universally salutary and indispensable, far less as any substitute for a practical hold upon Christianity and the Bible, or of at all comparable value with it. The user may even, if he likes, having in view the risks which beset practice from the misemployment of such criticism, say while he uses it that he is but making

himself friends through the mammon of unrighteous-
ness.

It is evident that the author of such criticism, holding
this to be its relation to the object of the Church of
England and to the business of the clergy, and holding
it so cheap by comparison with that object and that
business, is by no means constituted, through the fact of
his having published it, an enemy of the Church and
clergy, or precluded from feeling and expressing a hearty
desire for their preservation.

### 2.

I have called the Church of England,—to give the
plainest and most direct idea I could of its real reason
for existing,—*a great national society for the promotion of
goodness.* Nothing interests people, after all, so much as
goodness;[1] and it is in human nature that what interests
men very much they should not leave to private and
chance handling, but should give to it a public institution.
There may be very important things to which public
institution is not given; but it will generally turn out,
we shall find, that they are things of which the whole
community does not strongly feel the importance. Art

---

[1] 'We have no clear conception of any positive moral attribute
in the Supreme Being, but what may be resolved up into goodness.'—
Butler, in Sermon *Upon the Love of Our Neighbour.*

and literature are very important things, and art and
literature, it is often urged, are not matters of public
institution in England ; why, then, should religion be ?
The answer is, that so far as art and literature are not
matters of public institution like religion, this is because
the whole community has not felt them to be of vital
interest and importance to it, as it feels religion to be.
In only one famous community, perhaps, has the people
at large felt art and literature to be necessaries of life, as
with us the people at large has felt religion to be. That
community was ancient Athens. And in ancient Athens
art and literature were matters of public and national
institution, like religion. In the Christian nations of
modern Europe we find religion, alone of spiritual concerns, to have had a regular public organisation given to
it, because alone of spiritual concerns religion was felt
by every one to interest the nation profoundly, just like
social order and security.

It is true, we see a great community across the
Atlantic, the United States of America, where it cannot
be said that religion does not interest people, and
where, notwithstanding, there is no public institution
and organisation of religion. But that is because the
United States were colonised by people who, from
special circumstances, had in this country been led

to adopt the theory and the habit, then novel, of separatism ; and who carried the already formed theory and
habit into America, and there gave effect to it. The
same is to be said of some of our chief colonial depen-
dencies. Their communities are made up, in a remark-
ably large proportion, out of that sort and class of English
people in whom the theory and habit of separatism exist
formed, owing to certain old religious conflicts in this
country, already. The theory and the habit of separatism
soon make a common form of religion seem a thing both
impossible and undesirable ; and without a common form
of religion there cannot well be a public institution of it.
Still, all this does not make the public institution of a
thing so important as religion to be any the less the
evident natural instinct of mankind, their plain first impulse in the matter ; neither does it make that first
impulse to be any the less in itself a just one.

For a just one it is in itself, surely. All that is said to
make it out to be so, said by Butler for instance,—whom
I have already quoted, and whose practical view of things
is almost always so sound and weighty,—seems to me of an
evidence and solidity quite indisputable. The public institution of religion, he again and again insists, is ' a standing
publication of the Gospel,' ' a serious call upon men to
attend to it,' and therefore of an ' effect very important and

valuable.' A visible Church, with a publicly instituted
form of religion, is, he says, 'like a city upon a hill,—a
standing memorial to the world of the duty which we
owe our Maker ; to call men continually, both by example and instruction, to attend to it, and, by the form
of religion ever before their eyes. to remind them of the
reality ; to be the repository of the oracles of God ; to
hold up the light of revelation in aid to that of nature,
and to propagate it throughout all generations to the end
of the world.' ' That which men have accounted religion,'
he says again, in his charge to the clergy of Durham,
' has had, generally speaking, a great and conspicuous
part in all public appearances, and the face of it has been
kept up with great reverence throughout all ranks from
the highest to the lowest ; and without somewhat of this
nature, piety will grow languid even among the better
sort of men, and the worst will go on quietly in an abandoned course, with fewer interruptions from within than
they would have, were religious reflexions forced oftener
upon their minds, and, consequently. with less probability
of their amendment.' Here, I say, is surely abundant
reason suggested, if the thing were not already clear
enough of itself, why a society for the promotion of
goodness, such as the Church of England in its fundamental design is, should at the same time be a national

society, a society with a public character and a publicly instituted form of proceeding.

And yet with what enemies and dangers is this reasonable and natural arrangement now encompassed here ! I open the *Fortnightly Review* for the beginning of the present year,[1] in order to read the political summary, sure to be written with ability and vigour, and to find there what lines of agitation are in prospect for us. Well, I am told in the political summary that the disestablishment of the Church of England is ' a question which the very Spirit of Time has borne on into the first place.' The Spirit of Time is a personage for whose operations I have myself the greatest respect ; whatever he does, is, in my opinion, of the gravest effect. And he has borne, we are told, the question of the disestablishment of the Church of England into the very first rank of questions in agitation. ' The agitation,' continues the summarist, ' is the least factitious of any political movement that has taken place in our time. It is the one subject on which you are most certain of having a crowded meeting in any large town in England. It is the one bond of union between the most important groups of Liberals. Even the Tapers and Tadpoles of politics must admit that this party is rapidly becoming really formidable.'

[1] 1876.

Then our writer proceeds to enumerate the forces of his party. It comprises practically, he says, the whole body of the Protestant Noncomformists ; this is, indeed, a thing of course. But the Wesleyans, too, he adds, are almost certainly about to join it ; while of the Catholics it is calculated that two-thirds would vote for ' the policy of taking away artificial advantages from a rival hierarchy.'

' From within the Church itself,' he goes on, ' there are gradually coming allies of each of the three colours : Sacra- mentalists, weary of the Erastian bonds of Parliament and the Privy Council ; Evangelicals, exasperated by State connivance with a Romanising reaction ; Broad Churchmen, who are beginning to see, first, that a laity in a Free Church would hold the keys of the treasury, and would therefore be better able than they are now to secure liberality of doctrine in their clergy ; and, secondly, are beginning to see that the straining to make the old bottles of rite and formulary hold the wine of new thought withers up intellectual manliness, straightforwardness, and vigorous health of conscience, both in those who practise these economies and in those whom their moderation fascinates.

The thing could not well be more forcibly stated, and the prospect for the Established Church does indeed, as thus presented, seem black enough. But we have still to hear of the disposition of the great body of the flock, of the working multitudes. ' As for the working classes,' the writer says, ' the religious portion would follow the

M

policy of the sect to which the individual happened to belong ; while that portion which is not attached either to church or chapel, apart from personal or local considerations of accidental force, would certainly go for disestablishment. Not a single leader of the industrial class, with any pretence to a representative character, but is already strongly and distinctly pledged.' And the conclusion is, that ' the cause of disestablishment, so far from being the forlorn crusade of a handful of fanatics, is in fact a cause to which a greater number of Radicals of all kinds may be expected to rally than to any other cause whatever.' And therefore this cause should be made by all Liberals, the writer argues, the real object, and other things should be treated as secondary and contributory to it. ' Let us reform our electoral machinery,' says he, ' by all means, but let us understand, and make others understand, that we only seek this because we seek something else : the disestablishment of the Episcopal Church in England.' Such is the programme of what calls itself ' scientific liberalism.'

By far the most formidable force in the array of dangers which this critic has mustered to threaten the Church of England, is the estrangement of the working classes,—of that part of them, too, which has no attachment to Dissent, but which is simply zealous about social

and political questions. This part may not be over-
whelming in numbers, but it is the living and leading
part of the whole to which it belongs. Its sentiment tends
to become, with time, the sentiment of the whole. If its
sentiment is unalterably hostile to the Church of England,
if the character of the Church is such that this must
needs be so and remain so, then the question of disestablishment is, I think, settled. The Church of England
cannot, in the long run, stand.

The ideal of the working classes is a future,—a future
on earth, not up in the sky,—which shall profoundly
change and ameliorate things for them ; an immense
social progress, nay, a social transformation ; in short, as
their song goes, ' a good time coming.' And the Church
is supposed to be an appendage to the Barbarians, as I
have somewhere, in joke, called it ; an institution
devoted above all to the landed gentry, but also to
the propertied and satisfied classes generally ; favouring
immobility, preaching submission, and reserving transformation in general for the other side of the grave.

Such a Church, I admit, cannot possibly nowadays
attach the working classes, or be viewed with anything
but disfavour by them. But certainly the superstitious
worship of existing social facts, a devoted obsequious-
ness to the landed and propertied and satisfied classes,

does not inhere in the Christian religion. The Church
does not get it from the Bible. Exception is taken to its
being said that there is communism in the Bible, because
we see that communists are fierce, violent, insurrec-
tionary people, with temper and actions abhorrent to the
spirit of the Bible. But if we say, on the one hand, that
the Bible utterly condemns all violence, revolt, fierceness,
and self-assertion, then we may safely say, on the other
hand, that there is certainly communism in the Bible.
The truth is, the Bible enjoins endless self-sacrifice all
round ; and to any one who has grasped this idea, the
superstitious worship of property, the reverent devoted-
ness to the propertied and satisfied classes, is impossible.
And the Christian Church has, I boldly say, been the
fruitful parent of men who, having grasped this idea, have
been exempt from this superstition. Institutions are to
be judged by their great men ; in the end, they take their
line from their great men. The Christian Church, and
the line which is natural to it and which will one day
prevail in it, is to be judged from the saints and the tone
of the saints. Now really, if there have been any people
in the world free from illusions about the divine origin
and divine sanctions of social facts just as they stand,—
open, therefore, to the popular hopes of a profound renovation and a happier future,—it has been those inspired

idiots, the poets and the saints. Nobody nowadays attends much to what the poets say, so I leave them on one side. But listen to a saint on the origin of property ; listen to Pascal. ' " This dog belongs to *me*," said these poor children ; " that place in the sun is *mine !* " Behold the beginning and the image of all usurpation upon earth ! ' Listen to him instructing the young Duke of Roannez as to the source and sacredness of his rank and his estates. First, as to his estates :—

'Do you imagine,' he says, 'that it is by some way of nature that your property has passed from your ancestors to you? Such is not the case. This order is but founded on the simple will and pleasure of legislators, who may have had good reasons for what they did, but not one of their reasons was taken from any natural right of yours over these possessions. If they had chosen to ordain that this property, after having been held by your father during his lifetime, should revert to the commonwealth after his death, you would have had no ground for complaint. Thus your whole title to your property is not a title from nature, but a title of human creation. A different turn of imagination in the law-makers would have left you poor ; and it is only that combination of the chance which produced your birth with the turn of fancy producing laws advantageous to you, which makes you the master of all these possessions.'

And then, the property having been dealt with, comes the turn of the rank :—

There are two sorts of grandeurs in the world ; grandeurs

which men have set up, and natural grandeurs. The grandeurs which men have set up depend on the will and pleasure of men. Dignities and nobility are grandeurs of this kind. In one country they honour nobles, in another commoners ; here the eldest son, there the youngest son. Why ? because such has been men's will and pleasure.

There, certainly, speaks a great voice of religion without any superstitious awe of rank and of property ! The treasures of Pascal's scorn are boundless, and they are magnificent. They are poured out in full flood on the superstitious awe in question. The only doubt may be, perhaps, whether they are not poured out on it too cruelly, too overwhelmingly. But in what secular writer shall we find anything to match them ?

Ay, or in what saint or doctor, some one will say, of the Church of England ? If there is a stronghold of stolid deference to the illusions of the aristocratic and propertied classes, the Church of England, many people will maintain, is that stronghold. It is the most formidable complaint against ·the Church, the complaint which creates its most serious danger. There is nothing like having the very words of the complainants themselves in a case of this sort. 'I wish,' says Mr. Goldwin Smith, 'I wish the clergy would consider whether something of the decline of Christianity may not be due to the fact that for ages Christianity has been accepted by the clergy of the Established Church as the ally of political and social injustice.' 'The Church of England,' says Mr. John Morley, ' is the ally of tyranny, the organ of social oppression, the champion of intellectual bondage.' There are the leaders !—and the *Beehive* shall give us the opinion of the rank and file. ' The clergy could not take money from the employing classes and put it into the pockets of the employed ; but they might have insisted on such a humane consideration and Christian re-gard for human welfare, as would have so influenced men's dealings in regard to each other as to prevent our present misery and suffering.'

You will observe, by the way, and it is a touching thing to witness, that the complaint of the real sufferers, as they think themselves, is in a strain comparatively calm and mild ; how much milder than the invective of their literary leaders ! Still, the upshot of the complaint is the same with both. The Church shares and serves the pre-judices of rank and property, instead of contending with them.

Now, I say once more that every Church is to be judged by its great men. Theirs are the authoritative utterances. They survive. They lay hold, sooner or later, and in proportion to their impressiveness and truth, on the minds of Churchmen to whom they come down.

They strike the note to be finally taken in the Church. Listen, then, to this on ' the seemingly enormous discrimination,' as the speaker calls it, 'among men : '—

That distinction which thou standest upon, and which seemeth so vast, between thy poor neighbour and thee, what is it ? whence did it come ? whither tends it ?   It is not anywise natural, or according to primitive design.   Inequality and private interest in things (together with sicknesses and pains, together with all other infelicities and inconveniences) were the by-blows of our guilt ; sin introduced these degrees and distances ; it devised the names of rich and poor ; it begot those ingrossing and inclosures of things ; it forged those two small pestilent words, *meum* and *tuum*, which have engendered so much strife among men, and created so much mischief in the world ; these preternatural distinctions were, I say, brooded by our fault, and are in great part fostered and maintained thereby ; for were we generally so good, so just, so charitable as we should be, they could hardly subsist, especially in that measure they do.   God, indeed (for promoting some good ends and for prevention of some mischiefs apt to spring from our ill-nature in this our lapsed state, particularly to prevent the strife and disorder which scrambling would cause among men, presuming on equal right and parity of force), doth suffer them in some manner to continue ; but we mistake if we think that natural equality and community are in effect quite taken away ; or that all the world is so cantonised among a few that the rest have no share therein.

Who is it who says that ?   It is one of the eminently representative men of the English Church, its best and soundest moralist; a man sober-minded, weighty, esteemed ;—it is Barrow. And it is Barrow in the full blaze of the Restoration, in his Hospital Sermon of 1671.

Well, then, a fascinated awe of class-privileges, station, and property, a belief in the divine appointment, perfectness, and perpetuity of existing social arrangements, is not the authentic tradition of the Church of England. It is important to insist upon this, important for the Church to feel and avow it, because no institution with these prejudices could possibly carry the working classes with it. And it is necessary for the Church, if it is to live, that it should carry the working classes with it. Suffer me, after quoting to you Jeremy Taylor and Butler and Pascal and Barrow, to quote to you a much less orthodox personage : M. Renan. But what I am going to quote from him is profoundly true. He has been observing that Christianity, at its outset, had an immense attraction for the popular classes, as he calls them ; ‘ the popular classes whom the State and religion neglected equally.’ And he proceeds : ‘ Here is the great lesson of this history for our own age ; the times correspond to one another; the future will belong to that party which can get hold of the popular classes and elevate them.’ ‘ But in our days,’ M. Renan adds, ‘ the difficulty is far greater than it ever was.’ And this is true ; the difficulty

is great, very great.   But the thing has to be done, and
the Church is the right power to do it.

Now, the Church tends, people say, at present to
become more mixed and popular than it used to be in
the composition of its clergy.   They are recruited from a
wider field.   Sometimes one hears this lamented, and its
disadvantages insisted upon.   But, in view of a power of
comprehending popular ideals and sympathising with
them, it has, I think, its advantage.   No one can over-
look or deny the immense labours and sacrifices of the
clergy for the improvement of the condition of the
popular, the working classes ;—for their schools, for
instance, and for their physical well-being in countless
ways.   But this is not enough without a positive sympathy with popular ideals.   And the great popular ideal is,
as I have said, an immense renovation and transformation of things, a far better and happier society in the
future than ours is now.   Mixed with ail manner of alloy
and false notions this ideal often is, yet in itself it is
precious, it is true.   And let me observe, it is also the
ideal of our religion.   It is the business of our religion to
make us believe in this very ideal ; it is the business of
the clergy to profess and to preach it.   In this view it is
really well to consider, how entirely our religious teaching and preaching, and our creeds, and what passes with

us for 'the gospel,' turn on quite other matters from the
fundamental matter of the primitive gospel, or good news,
of our Saviour himself. This gospel was the ideal of
popular hope and longing, an immense renovation and
transformation of things : *the kingdom of God.* 'Jesus
came into Galilee proclaiming the good news of God and
saying : The time is fulfilled and the kingdom of God is
at hand ; repent and believe the good news.' Jesus
went about the cities and villages 'proclaiming the good
news of the kingdom.' The multitudes followed him,
and he 'took them and talked to them about the
kingdom of God.' He told his disciples to preach this.
'Go thou, and spread the news of the kingdom of God.'
'Into whatever city ye enter, say to them : The kingdom
of God has come nigh unto you.' He told his disciples to
pray for it,—to pray : 'Thy kingdom come!' He told them
to seek and study it before all things. 'Seek first God's
righteousness and kingdom.' He said that the news of it
should be published throughout the world. 'This good
news of the kingdom shall be proclaimed in the whole
world, for a witness to all nations.' And it was a kingdom
here on earth, not in some other world unseen. It was
'God's will done, as in heaven, so on earth.'

And in this line the preaching went on for some time
after our Saviour's death. Philip, in Samaria, 'delivers

the good news concerning the kingdom of God.' Paul,
at Ephesus, 'discusses and persuades concerning the
kingdom of God.' At Rome, he 'testifies to the kingdom
of God,' 'proclaims the kingdom of God.' He tells the
Corinthians that Christ sent him 'not to baptise but to
deliver the good news,'—the good news of the kingdom
of God. True, additions soon appear to the original
gospel, which explain how preaching came to diverge
from it. The additions were inevitable. The kingdom of
God was realisable only through Jesus,—was impossible
without Jesus. And therefore the preaching concerning
Jesus had necessarily to be added to the preaching
concerning the kingdom. Accordingly, we find Philip
'delivering the good news concerning the kingdom of
God, *and the name of Jesus Christ.*' We find him 'delivering (to the eunuch) the good news of *Jesus.*' We find
Paul 'proclaiming *Jesus, that he is the Son of God,*'
'proving *that he is the Christ,*' putting, as the foremost
matter of the ' good news,' Christ's death and resurrection.

'The kingdom' was to be won through faith in Christ;
in Christ crucified and risen, and crucified and risen, I
freely admit, in the plain material sense of those words.
And, moreover, 'the kingdom' was conceived by the
apostles as the triumphant return of Christ, in the lifetime of the very generation then living, to judge the

world and to reign in glory with his saints. The disciples conceived ' the kingdom,' therefore, amiss ; it was hardly possible for them not to do so. But we can readily understand how thus, as time went on, Christian preaching came more and more to drop, or to leave in the background, its one primitive gospel, *the good news of the kingdom*, and to settle on other points. Yet whoever reverts to it, reverts, I say, to the primitive *gospel* ; which is the good news of an immense renovation and transformation of this world, by the establishment of what the Sermon on the Mount calls (in the most authentic reading of the passage) ' God's righteousness and kingdom.' This was the ideal of Jesus :—the establishment on earth of God's kingdom, of felicity, not by the violent processes of our Fifth Monarchy men, or of the German Anabaptists, or of the French Communists, but by the establishment on earth of God's righteousness.

But it is a contracted and insufficient conception of the gospel which takes into view only the establishment of *righteousness*, and does not also take into view the establishment of *the kingdom*. And the establishment of the kingdom does imply an immense renovation and transformation of our actual state of things ;—that is certain. This then, which is the ideal of the popular classes, of the multitude everywhere, is a legitimate ideal.

And a Church of England, devoted to the service and ideals of any limited class,—however distinguished, wealthy, or powerful,—which is perfectly satisfied with things as they are, is not only out of sympathy with the ideal of the popular classes; it is also out of sympathy with the gospel, of which the ideal does, in the main, coincide with theirs. True, the most clear voice one could even desire in favour of such an ideal is found to come, as we have seen, from the Church of England, from a representative man among the clergy of that Church. But it is important that the clergy, as a body, should sympathise heartily with that ideal. And this they can best bring themselves to do, any of them who may require such bringing, by accustoming themselves to see that the ideal is the true original ideal of their religion and of its Founder.

I have dwelt a long while upon this head, because of its extreme importance. If the Church of England is right here, it has, I am persuaded, nothing to fear either from Rome, or from the Protestant Dissenters, or from the secularists. It cannot, I think, stand secure unless it has the sympathy of the popular classes. And it cannot have the sympathy of the popular classes unless it is right on this head. But, if it is right on this head, it may, I feel convinced, flourish and be strong with their sympathy, and with that of the nation in general. For it has natural allies in what Burke, that gifted Irishman, so finely calls ' the ancient and inbred integrity, piety, good nature, and good humour of the English people.' It has an ally in the English people's piety. If the matter were not so serious, one could hardly help smiling at the chagrin and manifest perplexity of such of one's friends as happen to be philosophical radicals and secularists, at having to reckon with religion again when they thought its day was quite gone by, and that they need not study it any more or take account of it any more, but it was passing out, and a kind of new gospel, half Bentham half Cobden, in which they were themselves particularly strong, was coming in. And perhaps there is no one who more deserves to be compassionated, than an elderly or middle-aged man of this kind, such as several of their Parliamentary spokesmen and representatives are. For perhaps the younger men of the party may take heart of grace, and acquaint themselves a little with religion, now that they see its day is by no means over. But, for the older ones, their mental habits are formed, and it is almost too late for them to begin such new studies. However, a wave of religious reaction *is* evidently passing over Europe ; due very much to our revolutionary and philosophical friends having insisted upon it that

religion was gone by and unnecessary, when it was
neither the one nor the other.   And what one sees in
France, and elsewhere, really makes some words of
Butler (if you are not yet tired of Butler) read like a
prophecy :—

'Indeed,' he says, 'amongst creatures naturally formed
for religion, yet so much under the power of imagination, so
apt to deceive themselves, as men are, superstition is an
evil which can never be out of sight.   But even against this,
true religion is a great security ; and the only one.   True
religion takes up that place in the mind which superstition
would usurp, and so leaves little room for it ; and likewise
lays us under the strongest obligations to oppose it.   On the
contrary, the danger of superstition cannot but be increased
by the prevalence of irreligion ; and by its general prevalence
the evil will be unavoidable.   For the common people,
wanting a religion, will of course take up with almost any
superstition which is thrown in their way ; and in process of
time, amidst the infinite vicissitudes of the political world,
the leaders of parties will certainly be able to serve themselves of that superstition, whatever it be, which is getting
ground ; and will not fail to carry it on to the utmost lengths
their occasions require.'

And does not one see at the present day, in the very places
where irreligion had prevailed most, superstition laying
hold of those who seemed the last people likely to be
laid hold of by it, and politicians making their game out
of this state of things?   Yet that there should spring up

in Paris, for instance, a Catholic Working Men's Union, and that it should prosper, will surprise no one who considers how strong is the need in human nature for a moral rule and bridle, such as religion, even a superstitious one, affords ; and how entirely the Paris workman was without anything of the kind.   La Rochefoucauld, who is here a witness whom no one will challenge, says most truly :  ' It is harder to keep oneself from being governed than to govern others.'   Obedience, strange as it may sound, is a real need of human nature;—above all, moral and religious obedience.   And it is less hard to a Paris workman to swallow beliefs which one would have thought impossible for him, than to go on in life and conduct in unchartered freedom, like a wave of the sea, driven with the wind and tossed.   Undoubtedly, then, there are in the popular classes of every country forces of piety and religion capable of being brought into an alliance with the Church, the national society for the promotion of goodness, in that country.   And of no people may this be more certainly said than of ours.

Still, there is in this English people an *integrity*, as Burke calls it,—a native fund of downrightness, plain honesty, integrity,—which makes our popular classes very unapt to cheat themselves in religion, and to swallow things down wholesale out of sentiment, or even out of

N

weariness of moral disorder and from need of a moral rule. And therefore I said that Rome was not a real danger for us, and that in the integrity of the English people the Church of England had a natural ally. I say this in view of the popular classes. Higher up, with individuals, and even with small classes, sentiment and fantasy, and morbid restlessness and weariness, may come in. But with the popular classes and with the English people as a whole, it is in favour of the Church that it is what Butler called it, and what it is sometimes reproached for being: a *reasonable* Establishment. And it *is* a reasonable Establishment, and in the good sense. I know of no other Establishment so reasonable. Churches are characterised, I have said, by their great men. Show me any other great Church of which a chief doctor and luminary has a sentence like this sentence, *splendide verax*, of Butler's : ‘Things are what they are, and the consequences of them will be what they will be ; why, then, should we desire to be deceived ? ’ To take in and to digest such a sentence as that, is an education in moral and intellectual veracity. And after all, intensely Butlerian as the sentence is, yet Butler came to it because he is *English* ; because at the bottom of his nature lay such a fund of integrity.

Show me another great Church, again, in which a

theologian, arguing that a religious doctrine of the truth
of which a man is not sure,—the doctrine, let us suppose, of a future state of rewards and punishments,—
may yet properly be made to sway his conduct and
practice (a recommendation which seems to me, I
must confess, impossible to be carried into effect) ; but
show me in another Church a theologian arguing thus,
yet careful at the same time to warn us, that we have no
business to tamper with our sense of evidence, by
*believing* the doctrine any the more on the ground of its
practical importance to us.    For this is what Butler says :
' To be influenced,' he says, ' by this consideration in
our *judgment*, to believe or disbelieve upon it, is indeed
as much prejudice as anything whatever.'    The force of
integrity, I say, can no farther go.            .

And, distracted as is the state of religious opinion
amongst us at this moment, in no other great Church is
there, I believe, so much sincere desire as there is in the
Church of England,—in clergy as well as in laity,—to get
at the real truth.    In no other great Church is there
so little false pretence of assured knowledge and
certainty on points where there can be none ; so
much disposition to see and to admit with Butler, in
regard to such points and to the root of the whole
matter in religion, that ' mankind are for placing the

N 2

stress of their religion anywhere rather than upon virtue,' and that mankind are wrong in so doing. To this absence of charlatanism, to this largeness of view, to this pressing to the genuine root of the matter, all the constituents assigned to the English people's nature by Burke,—our people's piety, their integrity, their good nature, their good humour, but above all, their *integrity*,— contribute to incline them. That the Church should show a like inclination, is in its favour as a National Church.

Equally are these constituents of the English cha- racter, and the way of thinking which naturally springs from them, in favour of the Church as regards the attacks of the political Dissenters. Plain directness of thinking, a largeness and good-naturedness of mind, are not favour- able judges, I think, for the Dissenters at the present moment,—for their grievances and for their operations. A sense of piety and religion in the nation is to be supposed to start with. And I suppose it to be clear that the contention no longer is, even on the part of the Dissenters themselves, that a certain Church-order is alone scrip- tural and is therefore necessary, and that it is that of the Dissenters, not of the Church ; or that the *Gospel* consists in one or two famous propositions of speculative doctrine, and that the Dissenters make it so to consist, while the Church does not. At any rate, the nation in general will no longer regard *this* contention as serious, even if some Dissenters do. The serious contention is, that there ought to be perfect religious equality, as it is called ; and that the State ought not to adopt, and by adopting to favour and elevate above the rest, one form of religion out of the many forms that are current.

But surely, the moment we consider religion and Christianity in a large way as goodness, and a Church as a society for the promotion of goodness, all that is said about having such a society before men's eyes as a city set upon a hill, all that is said about making the Gospel more and more a witness to mankind, applies in favour of the State adopting some form of religion or other, —that which seems best suited to the majority,—even though it may not be perfect ; and putting that forward as the national form of religion. 'A reasonable establishment *has*,' surely, as Butler says, 'a tendency to keep up a sense of real religion and real Christianity in a nation.' That seems to me to be no more than the plain language of common sense. And I think what follows is true also :—'And it is moreover necessary for the encouragement of learning, some parts of which the Scripture-revelation absolutely requires should be cultivated.'

But what seems to me quite certain is, that, it

goodness is the end, and 'all good men are,' as Butler
says, 'equally concerned in promoting that end,' then, as
he goes on to conclude, 'to do it more effectually they
ought to unite in promoting it ; which yet is scarce
practicable upon any new models, and quite impossible
upon such as every one would think unexceptionable.'
And as for such, he says, as 'think ours liable to objection, it is possible they themselves may be mistaken,
and whether they are or no, the very nature of society
requires some compliance with others.   Upon the whole,
therefore, these persons would do well to consider how
far they can with reason satisfy themselves in neglecting
what is certainly right on account of what is doubtful
whether it be wrong ; and when the right is of so much
greater consequence one way than the supposed wrong
can be the other.'   Here Butler seems to me to be on
impregnable ground, and it is the ground which the
largest and surest spirits amongst us have always pitched
upon.   Sir Matthew Hale, the most moderate of men
and the most disposed to comprehension, said : 'Those
of the separation were good men, but they had narrow
souls, who would break the peace of the Church about
such inconsiderable matters as the points in difference
were.'   Henry More, that beautiful spirit, is exactly to the
same effect.   'A little religion may make a man schis-

matical, but a great deal will surely make a man decline
division where things are tolerable, which is the case of
our English Church.' And the more a large way of
thinking comes to spread in this nation, which by its
good nature and good humour has a natural turn for it,
the more will this view come to prevail. It will be
acknowledged that the Church is a society for the promotion of goodness ; that such a society is the stronger
for being national, and ought to be national ; that to make
its operations, therefore, more effectual, all good men
ought to unite in it, and that the objections of the Protestant Dissenters to uniting in it are trivial.

At least, their *religious* objections to uniting in it
are trivial. Their objections from the annoyance and
mortification at having, after they have once separated
and set up forms of their own, to give in and to accept
the established form, and their allegations of their
natural jealousy at having to see, if they do not accept it,
the clergy preferred before them by being invested with
the status of national ministers of religion—these objections are much more worthy of note. But, in the first
place, whatever preference is given, is given for the sake
of the whole community, not of those preferred. And
many preferences, for its own sake and for what it judges
to be the public good, the whole community may and

must establish. But that which, as men's minds grow larger, will above all prevent the objections and complaints of the Dissenters from winning sympathy and from attaining effect, is that, in the second place, it will be more and more distinctly perceived that their objections and complaints are, to speak truly, *irreligious* objections and complaints, and yet urged in the sphere of religion.

To philosophical Radicals in or out of Parliament, who think that religion is all a chimæra, and that in a matter so little important the fancies of the Dissenters, whose political aid is valuable, may well be studied and followed, this will seem nothing. But the more the sense of religion grows, and of religion in a large way,—the sense of the beauty and rest of religion, the sense that its charm lies in its grace and peace,—the more will the present attitude, objections, and complaints of the Dissenters indispose men's minds to them. They will, I firmly believe, lose ground ; they will not keep hold of the new generations. In most of the mature Dissenters the spirit of scruple, objection-taking, and division, is, I fear, so ingrained, that in any proffered terms of union they are more likely to seize occasion for fresh cavil than occasion for peace. But the new generations will be otherwise minded. As to the Church's want of grace and peace in disputing the ground with Dissent, the justice of what Barrow says will be more and more felt : —'He that being assaulted is constrained to stand on his defence, may not be said to be in peace ; yet his not being so (involuntarily) is not to be imputed to him.' But the Dissenters have not this, the Church's excuse, for being men of war in a sphere of grace and peace. And they turn themselves into men of war more and more.

Look at one of the ablest of them, who is much before the public, and whose abilities I unfeignedly admire : Mr. Dale. Mr. Dale is really a pugilist, a brilliant pugilist. He has his arena down at Birmingham, where he does his practice with Mr. Chamberlain, and Mr. Jesse Collings, and the rest of his band ; and then from time to time he comes up to the metropolis, to London, and gives a public exhibition here of his skill. And a very powerful performance it often is. And the *Times* observes, that the chief Dissenting ministers are becoming quite the intellectual equals of the ablest of the clergy. Very likely ; this sort of practice is just the right thing for bracing a man's intellectual muscles. I have no fears concerning Mr. Dale's intellectual muscles ; what I am a little uneasy about is his religious temper. The essence of religion is grace and peace. And though, no doubt, Mr. Dale cultivates grace and peace at other times, when he is not busy with his anti-Church practice, yet his cultivation of grace and peace can be none the better, and must naturally be something the worse, for the time and energy given to his pugilistic interludes. And the more that mankind, instead of placing their religion in all manner of things where it is not, come to place it in sheer goodness, and in grace and peace,—and this is the tendency, I think, with the English people,— the less favourable will public opinion be to the proceedings of the political Dissenters, and the less has the Church to fear from their pugnacious self-assertion.

Indeed, to eschew self-assertion, to be,—instead of always thinking about one's freedom, and one's rights, and one's equality,—to be, as Butler says, 'as much afraid of subjection to mere arbitrary will and pleasure in ourselves as to the arbitrary will of others,' is the very temper of religion. What the clergy have to desire,—and the clergy of London may well bear to hear this, who have, as a body, been so honourably distinguished for their moderation and their intelligence,—what the clergy have to aim at, is the character of simple instruments for the public good. What they have to shun, is their action having at all the appearance of mere arbitrary will and pleasure of the individual. One can hardly speak about the Church at this moment without touching on the Burials Bill. Give me leave to say, that the dangerous

thing to the Church, as regards this vexed question of
Burials, has been the opening afforded, in the exclusion
of unbaptised persons, to the exercise of what might
always seem, and often was, the exercise of mere arbitrary will and pleasure in the individual clergyman.
This, it seems to me, ought certainly to be abandoned ;
and here, surely, is an occasion for remembering St.
Paul's dictum, that ' Christ sent him not to baptise, but
to preach the good news.' If this exclusion were wholly
abandoned, if the option of silent funerals, and of funerals with a shortened service, were also given, I think as
much would have been done as it is for the public
advantage (I put the advantage of the clergy out of
question altogether,—they have none but that of the
community), in the special circumstances of this country,
to do. I do not believe it would be necessary to do more,
in order to remove all real sense of grievance, and to
end, for sensible people, the need for further occupying
themselves with this whole barren and retarding question
of *Church and Dissent.*

And I, for my part, now leave this question, I hope,
for ever. I became engaged in it against my will, from
being led by particular circumstances to remark the
deteriorating effect of the temper and strifes of Dissent
upon good men, the lamentable waste of power and

usefulness which was thereby caused ; and from being convinced that the right settlement was to be reached in one way only : not by disestablishment, but by comprehension and union. However, as one grows old, one feels that it is not one's business to go on for ever expostulating with other people upon their waste of life, but to make progress in grace and peace oneself. And this is the real business of the Church too : to make progress in grace and peace. Force the Church of England has certainly some ; perhaps a good deal. But its true strength is in relying, not on its powers of force, but on its powers of attractiveness. And by opening itself to the glow of the old and true ideal of the Christian Gospel, by fidelity to reason, by placing the stress of its religion on goodness, by cultivating grace and peace, it will inspire attachment, to which the attachment which it inspires now, deep though that is will be as nothing ; it will last, be sure, as long as this nation.

## A LAST WORD ON THE BURIALS BILL.

IN my address at Sion College I touched for a moment on the now much-discussed question of the Burials Bill. I observed, that whatever resembled an arbitrary assertion of his own private will and pleasure should be shunned by a clergyman ; that the exercise of his right of refusing burial to unbaptised persons often resembled, and not unfrequently was, such an assertion ; and that it would be for the advantage of the Church to abandon this right.  I added that if this were done, and if the option of a silent service, or of a shortened service, in place of the present Burial Service, were also given, as much would have been conceded to the Dissenters, in the matter of burials, as justice requires, as much as it is for the public interest to concede, and as much as it will finally, I think, be found necessary to concede.

But much more than this is claimed for the Dissenters.  Mr. Osborne Morgan's Bill lays down, that ' it is just and right to permit the performance in parish churchyards of other burials than those of the Church of England, and by other persons than the ministers of that Church.' And the *Times* says in recommendation of Mr. Osborne Morgan's Bill :—

' A just legislature has to put the business on the basis of justice and truth. It will consider what a Dissenter or his friends desire, and what, being in accordance with his or their wishes, will be no injustice or untruth. It does really seem late in the day to have to prove that the imposition of a service at variance with the whole course of a man's life, opinions, and practice, is an injustice and an untruth. An Englishman has a right to worship in the style he thinks truest and best, just as he has a right to dress as he likes, to select his own acquaintances, or to choose his own pursuits. Let the Dissenting minister then,' concludes the *Times*, ' enter the churchyard, and have his own say over his own spiritual son or daughter ; and let the incumbent cease to intrench himself in the vain illusion of an inviolable church-yard in a parish which has long ceased to be his exclusive domain.'

Lord Selborne, too, in the debate on Lord Granville's resolution upon the subject of burials, treated it as a matter quite clear and self-evident, that to deny this right to Dissenters was a violation of the established English principle of religious liberty :—

' Is there any conceivable logical answer,' he asked, ' to the observation, that in these cases you deny after death that religious liberty which in every other respect is given to the deceased during the whole of their lives ? You deny this

liberty in the present state of things in two ways : by refusing
to them the liberty of being religious in their own way, and
by imposing upon them the necessity of being religious in
your way.' 'The feelings of the great majority of the laity,'
Lord Selborne adds, 'when it is brought home to them that
there is this violation of the established principle of religious
liberty in dealing with interments, will go more and more
with those who complain of this grievance.'

A number of clergymen, many of them bearing names
well-known and respected, have proposed, as 'a reasonable concession to the feelings of Nonconformists,' to
'grant permission to a recognised minister or representative of any religious body to perform in the churchyard a
funeral service consisting of passages of Holy Scripture,
prayers, and hymns.' But absolute liberty is the right
claimed, and these limitations are evidently inconsistent
with it. 'We are afraid,' says the *Times* of the clergymen's proposal, 'that even with the most liberal interpretation, this restriction leaves out of account some communities for whose rights the supporters of the Bill would
contend as strenuously as for those of others. *But it is a
misapprehension, it is to be apprehended, of the essential
nature of a Nonconformist, to suppose that he would ever
pledge himself to conform to anything.* The essence of his
demand is to claim free access to sacred places, which
the necessity of nature compels him to use, with such

observances as the principles of his communion may prescribe.' Yes, 'necessity of nature.' For, it is argued,
'while every other public incident of a man's life must
be optional, he must be buried.' And therefore, contends
the *Times* to exactly the same effect as Lord Selborne,
' let the natural necessity of burial be once admitted, and
the necessity of according religious freedom in the satisfaction of it must inevitably be allowed.'

Finally, it is said that in all other Christian countries,
except Spain, the right of burying their dead in the parish
churchyard, with their own services and their own ministers, is conceded to Dissenters. And here again, then,
is a reason why in England too the clergyman should, as
the *Times* says, ' cease to intrench himself in the vain
illusion of an inviolable churchyard in a parish which has
long ceased to be his exclusive domain ; ' should ' let the
Dissenting minister enter the ground, and have his own
say over his own spiritual son or daughter.'

I have been asked, how the concession which I spoke
of at Sion College can be thought sufficient, when it is so
much less than what the Dissenters themselves and their
friends demand, than what some of the best of the clergy
offer to concede, than what natural justice and the
recognised English principle of religious liberty require,
and than what is almost universally conceded in the rest

of Christendom ? And I am asked this by those who approach the question, just as I approach it myself, in a spirit perfectly disinterested. They, like myself, have no political object to serve by answering it in a way favourable to the Dissenters, they do not care whether or not it is the liberal-looking, popular, taking thing so to answer it. And, on the other hand, they have no need to bid for the support of the clergy; they are, moreover, without the least touch of ecclesiastical bias. They simply want to get the question answered in a way to satisfy their own minds and consciences, want to find out what is really the right and reasonable course to pursue. And for their satisfaction, and also for my own, I return for a moment to this matter of burials, before finally leaving the whole question of Church and Dissent ; that I may not seem to be leaving it with a curt and inconsiderate judgment on a matter where the feelings of the Dissenters are strongly interested.

2.

What is the intention of all forms of public ceremonial and ministration ? It is, that what is done and said in a public place, and bears with it a public character, should be done and said worthily. The public is responsible for it. The public gets credit and advantage from it if it is done worthily, is compromised and harmed by it if it is done

o

unworthily. The mode, therefore, of performing public functions in places invested with a public character is not left to the will and pleasure of chance individuals. It is expressly designed to rise above the level which would be thence given. If there is a sort of ignobleness and vulgarity (*was uns alle bändigt, das Gemeine*) which comes out in the crude performance of the mass of mankind left to themselves, public forms, in a higher strain and of recognised worth, are designed to take the place of such crude performance. They are a kind of schooling, which may educate gradually such performance into something better, and meanwhile may prevent it from standing forth, to its own discredit and to that of all of us, as public and representative. This, I say, is evidently the design of all forms for public use on serious and solemn occasions. No one will say that the common English-man glides off-hand and by nature into a strain pure, noble, and elevated. On the contrary, he falls with great ease into vulgarity. But no people has shown more attachment than the English to old and dignified forms calculated to save us from it.

Such is the origin and such is the defence of the use of a set form of burial-service in our public churchyards. It stands on the same ground as the use of all appointed · forms whatever, in public places and on serious occasions. It is designed to save public places and occasions, and to save our character as a community, from being discredited through what the caprice and vulgarity of individuals might prompt them to. The moment a place has a public and national character, there emerges the requirement of a public form for use there. And therefore it is really quite marvellous to find a man of Lord Selborne's acuteness maintaining, that to withhold from the Dissenting minister the right, as the *Times* says, 'to enter the churchyard and have his own say over his own spiritual son or daughter,' is 'to deny after death that religious liberty, which in every other respect is given to the deceased during the whole of their lives.' To be sure, Lord Selborne was speaking in a parliamentary debate, where perhaps it is lawful to employ any fallacy which your adversaries cannot at the moment expose. But is it possible that Lord Selborne can himself have been deceived by the argument, that to refuse to Dissenters the liberty to have what services they please performed over them in the parish churchyard, is to 'deny after death that religious liberty, which in every other respect is given to the deceased during the whole of their lives'? True, the deceased have had religious liberty during their lives, have been free to choose what religious services they pleased. But where? In private places. They have no more been free, during their lifetime, to have what proceedings they liked in the parish church and in the parish churchyard, than to have what proceedings they liked in the House of Lords or in the Court of Chancery. And for the same reason in each case : that these places are public places, and that to safeguard the worthy use of public places we have public forms.

That liberty, then, in his choice of religious proceedings, which the deceased Dissenter enjoyed during his lifetime, or which any Englishman enjoys, is a liberty exercisable only in private places. The Dissenter, like other people, enjoys just the same liberty after his death. To refuse to any and every individual the liberty to dictate after his death what shall be done and said in a place set apart for national use, and belonging to the public, is just the same abridgment of his religious liberty,—as much and as little an abridgment of it,—as he has been subjected to during the whole course of his life. He has never during his whole life been free to have, in such a place, whomsoever he likes 'enter the ground and have his own say.' He is not free to have it after his death.

It is impossible to establish a distinction between a man's rights in regard to his burial, and his rights in regard to other public incidents, as they are called, of his life. They are optional, it is sometimes said ; burial is necessary. Even were this true, it would prove nothing as to a need for exemption in burial, rather than in other matters, from the requirement of public forms in public places. Burial is necessary, but not burial in public places. But the proposition is practically not true. For practical purposes, and in regard to mankind in general, it is not true that marriage is optional. It is not even true that religious worship is optional. Human nature being what it is, and society being what it is, religious worship and marriage may both of them, like burial, be called necessary. They come in the regular course of things and engage men's sentiments widely and deeply. And everything that can be said about the naturalness of a man's wishing to be buried in the parish churchyard by a minister of his own persuasion and with a service to his own liking, may be said about the naturalness of his wishing to be married in the parish church in like fashion. And the same of worshipping in the parish church. It is natural that a man should wish to enjoy, in his own parish church, worship of his own choice, conducted by a minister of his own selecting. And the hearty believers in a man's natural right to have in the parish churchyard a burial to his own liking, do not conceal that they believe also in a man's natural right to have in the parish

church a worship to his own liking. 'Let me be honest
about it,' said Sir Wilfrid Lawson at Carlisle ; 'if you let
the Nonconformist into the churchyard, that is only a
step towards letting him into the church.' The two
rights do, in fact, stand on precisely the same footing.
If the naturalness of a man's wishing for a thing creates
for him a right to do it, then a Dissenter can urge his
right to have his own minister say his say over him in
the parish churchyard. Equally can he urge his right to
have his own minister say his say to him in the parish
church.

What bars the right is in both cases just the same
thing : the higher right of the community. For the credit
and welfare of the community, public forms are appointed
to be observed in public places. The will and pleasure of
individuals is not to have sway there. This is what bars
the Nonconformist's right to have in his life-time what
minister and service he likes in the parish church. It is
also what bars his right to have after his death what
minister and service he likes in the parish churchyard.

Certain clergymen have been arbitrary, insolent, and
vexatious, in exercising the power given to them by that
rubric which excludes unbaptised persons from a legal
claim to the burial-service of the Church of England. I
can understand people being provoked into a desire to

'give a lesson,' as Lord Coleridge said, to such clergymen, by admitting Dissenting ministers to perform
burial-services in the churchyard.   I can understand the
better spirits among the clergy being disposed, out of
shame and regret at the doings of some of their brethren,
to concede to Dissenters what they desire in the matter
of burials.   I can understand their being disposed to
concede it, too, out of love of peace, and from the
wish to end disputes and to conciliate adversaries by
abandoning a privilege.   But the requirement of a fixed
burial-service in the parish churchyard is not made for
the benefit of the clergy, or in order to confer upon the
clergy a privilege.   It is made for the benefit of the
community.   It is not to be abandoned out of resentment against those who abuse it, or out of generosity on
the part of the more liberal clergy.   They are generous
with what is really, however it may appear to them, not a
privilege of theirs, but a safeguard of ours.   If it is for
the advantage of the community that in public places
some public form should be followed, if the community
runs risk of discredit from suffering individuals to say
and do what they like in such places, and if the burial-
service of the Church of England is enjoined on this
principle, then it is not to be given up in order to punish
the folly of some of the clergy or to gratify the generosity

of others. If the principle on which it has been en-joined is sound, the service is to be retained for the sake of this principle.

And so evidently sound is the principle, that the politicians who take the Dissenters' cause in hand cannot help feeling its force. Mr. Osborne Morgan proposes, while allowing the Dissenters to have their own services in the parish churchyard, to ' make proper provision for order and decency.' Lord Granville stipulates that the services shall be conducted 'in an orderly and Christian manner.' But unless these are mere words, meant to save appearances but not to have any real operation, we are thus brought back to the use of some public and recognised form for burials in the parish churchyard. And the burial-service of the Church of England was meant for a public and recognised form of this kind, which people at large could accept, and which ensured an 'orderly and Christian' character to proceedings in the parish churchyard. Proceedings dependent solely on the will and pleasure of chance individuals, and liable to bear the marks of their ' natural taste for the bathos,' as Swift calls it, cannot ensure this character. But proceedings in a public place ought to have it. And that they ought, the very politicians who advocate the Dissenters' cause admit.

So it is a case for revision of the public form of burial at present imposed. The burial-service of the Prayer-Book was meant to be used in the parish church-yard over all Christians,—meant to suit all. It does not suit all. Some people object to things in the service itself. More object to being strictly confined to that service only. More still object to being deprived, in their burial, of the offices of a minister of their own persuasion. On the other hand, a self-willed clergyman is enabled by a rubric of the burial-service to withhold its use in some cases where its use is desired, and where to withhold it is both foolish and cruel. Such is the present state of things. And it has to be dealt with by means of some change or other, which shall remove causes for just discontent, without abandoning the principle of requiring proper and worthy forms to be observed at proceedings in the parish churchyard.

3.

There is division among Christians, and in no country are they found all agreeing to adopt the same forms and ministers of religion. Different bodies of Christians have their own forms and ministers. And except in England these different bodies have, it is said, the churchyard in common. In Ireland it is so. In Scotland there is, as in England, an Established Church ; yet in

Scotland the forms and ministers of other religious bodies are admitted to the use of the parish churchyard. In France the Catholics are in an enormous majority, yet Protestants can be buried with their own forms in the graveyards of Catholic churches. In Germany, where both Catholics and Protestants are found in great numbers, and much intermixed, the churchyards of the one confession are open to the burial-rites of the other.

Now, in comparing the Church of England with other Churches, it is right to remember one character which distinguishes it from all of them. The Church of England was meant, in the intention of those who settled it at the Reformation, to satisfy the whole English people and to be accepted by them. It was meant to include both Catholics and Protestants in a compromise between old and new, rejecting Romish corruptions and errors, but retaining from Catholicism all that was sound and truly attaching, and thus to provide a revised form of religion, adapted to the nation at large as things then stood, and receivable by it. No other Church has been settled with the like design. And therefore no other Church stands precisely on the like ground in offering its formularies to people. For whereas other Churches, in offering their formularies to people, offer them with the recommendation that here is truth and everywhere else is error, the

Church of England, in offering its formularies to
Englishmen, offers them with the recommendation that
here is truth presented expressly so as to suit and unite
the English nation. And therefore to no Church can
dissent be so mortifying as to the Church of England ;
because dissent is the denial, not only of her profession
of the truth, but also of her success in her direct design.
However, this cannot make things otherwise than they
are. The Church of England, whatever may have
been its design, does not manage to satisfy every one
any more than the Churches in other countries. And
whatever special mortification she may have cause for,
in seeing, around her, forms and ministers of religion
other than her own, that is no reason why she should be
less liberal in her dealings with them than the Churches
in other countries. Either she must manage to suit them
herself, or she must be liberal to them.

Reciprocity, at any rate, is but fair. If the burial-
rites of the Church of England are admitted to Presbyterian churchyards in Scotland, and to Catholic churchyards in Ireland, the burial-rites of Scotch Presbyterians
and of Irish Catholics ought surely to be admitted to
Anglican churchyards. There can be no fear that the
burial-rite of either should do discredit to the churchyard.
The funerals of Scotch Presbyterians are conducted, I

believe, in silence. In a silent interment there can be nothing offensive. The Catholic offices for the dead are the source from whence our own are taken. In either case we have the security for decency which the deliberate public consent of large and well-known bodies of our fellow Christians affords on behalf of the burial-rites in use with them. Great bodies, like these, are not likely to have given their sanction to a form of burial-service discreditable to a public churchyard and inadmissible there. And if we had only to deal with the Presbyterians and the Catholics, the burials question would present itself under conditions very different from those which now do actually attend it. Nay, if the English Dissenters were reducible, even, to a few great divisions, —suppose to the well-known three denominations,—and either there were a common form of burial-service among these denominations, or each denomination had its own; and if the Dissenters were content to be thus classed, and to adhere either to a single form of Dissenters' burial-service, or to one out of two or three; then, also, the case would be different.

But these are not the conditions under which we are dealing with the burials question. The dissidence of Dissent and the Protestantism of the Protestant religion have brought the Dissenters in England to classify them-

selves, not in two or three divisions, but in, I believe, one
hundred and thirty-eight. And their contention is, that no
matter how they may split themselves up, they have still
their right to the churchyard ;—new sects as much as old,
small sects as much as great, obscure sects as much as
famous ; Ranters, Recreative Religionists, and Peculiar
People, as much as Presbyterians and Baptists. And no
man is entitled to tell them that they must manage to agree
among themselves upon one admissible form of burial-
service or upon one or two admissible forms. That
would be restricting their religious liberty. ' It is a misapprehension,' the *Times,* their advocate, tells us, ' of the
essential nature of a Nonconformist, to suppose that he
could ever pledge himself to conform to anything. The
essence of his demand is to claim free access to sacred
places, which the necessity of nature compels him to use,
with such observances as the principles of his communion
may prescribe.' Whether the observances are seemly,
and such as to befit a public and venerable place, we are
not to ask. Probably the Dissenters themselves think
that a man's conscience recommending them to him
makes them so. And what Lord Granville and Mr.
Osborne Morgan and the political friends of the Dissenters think on this matter, and how they propose to
ensure the decent and Christian order for which they

stipulate, and at the same time not to violate that essential principle of a Nonconformist's nature which forbids him in religion ' ever to pledge himself to conform to anything,' does not quite appear. Perhaps they have not looked into the thing much. Or they may think that it does not matter much, and that the observances of one body of religionists are likely to be about as good as those of another.

Yet surely there is likely to be a wide difference between the observances of a great body like the Presbyterians, counting its adherents by hundreds of thousands, having existed for a long time, and possessing a well-known reason for existence,—counting, also, amongst its adherents, a great mass of educated people,— there is likely to be a wide difference between the observances of a body like this, and the observances of such a body, say, as the Peculiar People. Both are Dissenters in England. But one affords the same sort of security, that its proceedings in a parish churchyard will be decorous, which Anglicanism itself affords. The other affords no such security at all. And it is precisely in the country churchyards, if accessible to them, that the observances of ignorant and fanatical little sects would parade themselves ; for these sects are found above all in country places, where there are no cemeteries, and not

in great towns, where these are. And we are not to take
security against such a violation of the parish churchyard,
by requiring the hundred and thirty-eight Dissenting
sects to agree to one or more authorisable forms of burial-
service for themselves, if they object to the burial-service
of the Church of England, because, where religious
observances are concerned, 'it is the essential nature of
a Nonconformist not to pledge himself to conform to
anything !' But the Nonconformist's pretension, to be
dispensed from pledging himself thus, can only be allowed
so long as he is content to forego, in exercising it, the
use of places with a public and national character. To
admit such a pretension in those using, for any purpose,
a place with a public and national character, is a mere
plunge into barbarism.

The example of foreign countries is quoted, and of
the foreign countries most like our own, France and
Germany. In France there are many churchyards with
a separate portion for Protestants, and in this separate
portion Protestants are buried with their own rites and
by their own ministers. This, as has been pointed out, is
not what our Dissenters wish for or would accept. In
Germany there is no such separation, and Protestants are
buried in Catholic churchyards by their own ministers,
with their own rites. But, in either case, *what* Pro-

testants? In France, Protestants belonging to the Reformed, or Calvinistic, Church; a Church with a great history, a Church well known, with a well-known rite, and paid and recognised by the State equally with the Catholic Church. In Germany, Protestants belonging to the Lutheran Church, to the Calvinistic Church, and to the Church formed by the union of the two. Like the Reformed Church in France, these are all of them public bodies, with a public status, a recognised rite, and offering sound security for their proper use of a public place like the churchyard. Do English people imagine that in France or Germany, whose liberality is vaunted at the expense of ours, Ranters or Recreative Religionists or Peculiar People are all of them free to 'have their say' in the parish churchyards? Do they imagine that in the use, such as it is, of Catholic churchyards by Protestants in France and Germany, the 'essential principle' of our English Nonconformist, 'not to pledge himself to conform to anything,' is allowed to have sway? If they do, they are very much mistaken.

Nothing, therefore, in the example of France and Germany condemns the taking a security from those who are admitted to use their burial-rites in the parish churchyard. If Catholics and the three Dissenting denominations were admitted, each with a recognised burial-

service, to our churchyards, that would be, in a general
way, a following of the precedent set by France and
Germany;—at any rate, of the precedent set by Germany.
But to this the Nonconformists themselves will never
consent, therefore it is idle to propose it.    And there are
other reasons, too, for not proposing such an arrangement in this country.    In the first place, it is not
required in order to ensure religious burial for Christians
of all kinds.    The Church of England, as has been
already said, was expressly meant to serve the needs of
the whole community.    And speaking broadly and generally, one may say that the whole Christian community
has at present a legal right to her burial-offices, and does
obtain them.    The Catholic Church does not bury
Protestants, but the Church of England buries Protestants and Catholics alike.    Then, too, the mass of the
Protestant Dissenters use the burial-service of the Church
of England without objection. .   And the country is
accustomed from of old to see used in the parish churchyards this burial-service only, and to see it performed by
the clergyman only.    Public feeling would certainly be
displeased by a startling innovation in such a matter,
without urgent need.    And there is no urgent need.
Again, there is certainly a danger that Catholics, their
position towards the Church of England being what it is,

P

might be disposed, if they were admitted with their ceremonies to the parish churchyards, to make capital, as the phrase is, out of that event, to render it subservient to farther ends of their own. And this danger does not exist on the Continent, for there the Catholics stand towards no Protestant Church in the position which here they hold towards the Church of England. It does not exist in Scotland, where the Established Church is not (I may say it, I hope, as I mean it, without offence) a sufficiently great affair to tempt Catholics to make capital out of the admission of their rites to the parish churchyards. All this would incline one to keep the practice as to burials in the main as it is now, in the English churchyards, unless there is some clear hardship in it.

Such a hardship is found by some people in the mere fact of not being free to choose one's own rite and one's own minister. As to the free choice of rite in a public place, enough has been said ; and it is admitted that in itself the burial-rite of the Church of England is not generally unacceptable. There remains the hardship of not being able to have one's own minister to bury one. The language used by Lord Granville on this topic was surprising. No doubt, the feelings may be soothed and pleased by the thought that the service over one's remains will be performed by a friend and acquaintance, not by a stranger. But to say that the sentiment demanding this satisfaction is so deep and natural that its demands must without fail be obeyed, and that much ought to be sacrificed in order to enable us to obey them, is really ridiculous. From the nature of things, such a sentiment cannot generally be indulged. Life and its chances being what they are, to expect that the minister, whose services we require to bury us, shall be at the same time a friend or acquaintance, shall be at any rate a man of our own choosing, is extravagant. That the form fixed for him to follow in ministering over us shall in itself be proper and acceptable, is the great matter. This being once secured, the more we forget the functionary in the service, the better. The Anglican burial-service has a person appointed to read it : the parish clergyman. In itself, the Anglican burial-service is considered, by the great majority of Protestant Dissenters, fit and acceptable. And it is taken, almost every word of it, from the Catholic offices of religion, the old common form of worship for Christendom. For a national Christian burial-service this is surely enough. The service is both approved and approvable. But Lord Granville's sentiment, it seems, is wounded, unless he may also approve the minister who is to read it over him. I should never have credited him with so much scrupulosity.

A parishioner's right to be buried in the parish churchyard, with this approved and approvable burial-service, is what we really have to guard. The real grievance is when this right is infringed. It is occasionally infringed, and infringed very improperly and vexatiously. The means for infringing it are afforded by the rubric prefixed to the burial-service, a rubric directing that ' the office ensuing is not to be used for any that die unbaptised, or excommunicate, or have laid violent hands upon themselves.' Excommunication is no longer practised. To refuse the burial-office to suicides is a penal measure, in the abstract perhaps consonant with public opinion, practically, however, in all but extreme cases, evaded by treating the suicide as of unsound mind. In the denial of the burial-office to ' any that die unbaptised ' lies the true source of grievance.

The office is meant for Christians, and this was what the rubric intended, no doubt, to mark ; baptism being taken as the stamp common to all Christians. But a large and well-known sect of Christians, the Baptists, defer baptism until the recipient is of adult age, and their children, therefore, if they die, die unbaptised. To inquire whether a child presented for burial is a Baptist's child or not, is an inquiry which no judicious and humane clergyman would make. The office was meant for

Christians, and Baptists are Christians, for surely they do not cease to be so because of their tenet of adult baptism. Adult baptism was undoubtedly the primitive usage, although the change of usage adopted by the Church was natural and legitimate, and the sticklers (as may so often be said of the sticklers in these questions) would have been wiser had they acquiesced in it. But the rubric dresses the clergyman in an authority for investigating and excluding, which enables a violent and unwise man to play tricks that might, indeed, make the angels weep. Where he has the law on his side, he can refuse the burial-service outright to innocent infants and children the most piously brought up ; he can, under pretence of doubt and inquiry, adjourn, and often withhold it, where he has not.

Such a man does harm to the Church ; but it is not likely that he will have the sense to see this, when he has not eyes to see what harm he does to himself. There may not be many of such men, but a few make a great noise, and do a great deal of mischief. There is no stronger proof of the immense power of inspiring attachment which the Church of England possesses, and of the lovable and admirable qualities shown by many of the clergy, than that the Church should still have so strong a hold upon the affections of the country, in spite of such mischief-makers. If the Church ever loses it and is broken up, it will be by their fault. It was the view of this sort of people with their want of temper and want of judgment, the view of their mischievous action, exerting itself with all the pugnacity and tenacity of the British character, and of their fatal prominence, which moved Clarendon, a sincere friend of the Church of England, to that terrible sentence of his : ' Clergymen, who understand the least, and take the worst measure of human affairs, of all mankind that can write and read ! '

The truly desirable, the indispensable change in the regulation of burials, is to remove the power of doing mischief which such persons now enjoy. And the best way to remove it, is to strike out the first rubric to the burial-service altogether. Excommunicated persons there are none to exclude. What is gained by insisting on the exclusion of suicides? In nine cases out of ten, the plea of unsound mind is at present used to prevent their exclusion, from the natural feeling that to exclude them is really to visit their offence, not upon them, but upon their relations and friends,—to punish the living for the fault of the dead. Where ought the widest latitude of merciful construction to be more permitted, where ought rigidity in sentencing, condemning, and excluding to be more discouraged, than in giving or withholding Christian burial? Of the test of baptism we have just now spoken.

It was meant as a test of the Christian profession of those buried in a Christian churchyard. The test excludes many whose Christian profession is undoubted. But with regard to this profession, again, where is the virtue of being jealously critical after a man's death and when he is brought for burial? What good end can be served by severity here, what harm prevented? Those who were avowedly and notoriously not Christians, will, it may be supposed, have forbidden their friends to bring them for Christian burial. If their friends do bring them, that is in fact to recant on behalf of the dead his errors, and to make him profess Christianity. Surely the Church can be satisfied with that, so far, at least, as not to refuse him burial! But, in fact, the great majority of those who reject Christianity, and who openly say so, have nevertheless been baptised, and cannot be excluded from Christian burial. Can it be imagined, that the mere rite of baptism is a rite the non-performance of which on a man during his lifetime makes the Christian burial of him, after his death, a vain and impious mockery? Yes, clergymen can be found who imagine even this. Clergymen write and print that their conscience will not suffer them to pronounce words of hope over an unbaptised person, because Jesus Christ said: 'Except a man be born of water and of the Spirit, he cannot enter into the kingdom

of God.' Perhaps no vagaries in the way of misinterpretation of Scripture-texts ought to cause surprise, the thing
is so common. But this misinterpretation of Jesus Christ's
words is peculiarly perverse, because it makes him say
just the very opposite of what he meant to say. ' Except
a man *be cleansed and receive a new influence,*' Jesus
meant to say, 'he cannot enter into the kingdom of God.'
And St. Peter explains what this *being cleansed* is : ' The
answer of a good conscience towards God,'—of which
baptism is merely the figure. Reliance on miracles,
reliance on supposed privileges, reliance on external rites
of any kind, are exactly what our Saviour meant, in the
words given in the Fourth Gospel, to condemn ;—reliance
on anything, except an interior change.

The rubric in question, therefore, might with advantage
be expunged altogether. If clergymen complain that
they shall then be compelled to pronounce words of
hope and assurance in cases where it is shocking, and a
mere mockery, to use them, it is to be said that this they
are just as much compelled to do now. But no doubt
such a necessity ought not to be imposed upon the clergy.
And in some cases, so long as the service stands as it
does now, it *is* imposed upon them, and this equally
whether the rubric is struck out or not. The words
expressing good hope concerning the particular person

buried impose it. But perhaps what has been said of
the unadvisableness of using the occasion of burial for
passing sentence of condemnation or pronouncing an
opinion *against* the particular person dead, is true also,
though certainly in a much less degree, of using it for
pronouncing an opinion in his favour. We are intruding
into things too much beyond our ken. At any rate, even
though the bystanders, who know the history of the
departed, may well in their hearts apply specially to him
the hopes and promises for the righteous, the general
burial-service has another function. It moves in a higher
region than this region of personal application. Its
grandeur lies in its being a service over *man* buried.
'We commit his body to the ground in the sure and
certain hope of the resurrection to eternal life,' is exactly
right. *The* resurrection, not this or that individual's
resurrection. We affirm our sure and certain hope, that
for *man* a resurrection to eternal life there is. To add
anything like a pronouncement concerning this or that
man's special share in it, is not the province of a general
service. The words, 'as our hope is this our brother
doth,' would really be better away. For the sake of the
service itself, its truth, solemnity, and impressiveness,
they would be better away. And if they were away,
there would be removed with them a source of shock

and distress to the conscience of the officiating clergyman, which exists now, and which, he might say, would exist even more were the introductory rubric expunged.

The requirement of a fixed and noble form, consecrated by use and sentiment, as the national burial-service in our parish churchyards, is a thing of the highest importance and value. Speech-making and prayer-making, substitutions or additions of individual invention, hazarded *ex tempore*, seem to me unsuitable and undesirable for such a place and such an occasion. In general, what it is sought to give utterance to by them can find its proper expression in the funeral-sermon at another time. With hymns the case is different. They are not inventions made off-hand by individuals round the grave. We at least know what they will be, and we are safe in them from the incalculable surprises and shocks of a speech or an outpouring. Hymns, such as we know them, are a sort of composition which I do not at all admire. I freely say so now, as I have often said it before. I regret their prevalence and popularity amongst us. Taking man in his totality and in the long run, bad music and bad poetry, to whatever good and useful purposes a man may often manage to turn them, are in themselves mischievous and deteriorating to him. Somewhere and somehow, and at some time or other, he

has to pay a penalty and to suffer a loss for taking delight
in them. It is bad for people to hear such words and such
a tune as the words or tune of, *O happy place ! when shall
I be, my God, with thee, to see thy face?*—worse for them to
take pleasure in it. And the time will come, I hope,
when we shall feel the unsatisfactoriness of our present
hymns, and they will disappear from our religious services.
But that time has not come yet, and will not be brought
about soon or suddenly. We must deal with circumstances as they exist for us. Hymns are extremely popular
both with Church-people and with Dissenters. Church
and Dissent meet here on a common ground ; and both
of them admit, in hymns, an element a good deal less
worthy, certainly, than the regular liturgy, but also a good
deal less fixed. In the use of hymns we have not, then,
as in the use of speeches and extemporaneous prayings, a
source of risk to our public religious services from which
they are at present free ; for they allow of hymns already.
Here are means for offering, without public detriment, a
concession to Dissenters, and for gratifying their wishes.
Many of them would like, in burying their friends, to
sing a hymn at the grave. Let them. Some concession
has been already proposed in the way of allowing a
hymn to be sung as the funeral enters the churchyard.
Let the concession be made more free and ample ; let a

hymn or hymns be admitted as a part of the regular service at the grave. The mourners should have to give notice beforehand to the clergyman of their wish for the hymn, and it ought to be taken from one of the collections in general use.

This hymnody would lengthen the burial-service. In view of this, I should like to suggest one alteration in that beautiful and noble service; an alteration by which time might be got for the hymn when desired, and which would moreover in itself be, I cannot but think, an improvement. The burial-service has but one lesson, taken out of the fifteenth chapter of the First Epistle to the Corinthians. The passage taken is very long, and, eloquent and interesting as it is, yet it is also, as a whole, very difficult to understand. I should say that it is difficult as a whole because as a whole it is embarrassed, were it not that many people cannot conceive of an inspired writer as ever embarrassed. I will not raise questions of this kind now. But difficult the lesson certainly is; difficult, and also very long. Yet it has parts which are most grand and most edifying; and which also, taken by themselves, are quite clear. And a lesson of Scripture should make, as far as possible, a broad, deep, simple, single impression; and it should bring out that impression quite clear. Above all, a lesson used at the burial of the dead, and with the hearers' minds affected as they then are, should do this. It should be a real *lesson*, not merely a *lection* ; which,—from our habit of taking for this purpose long readings, hardly ever less than an entire chapter, and in which many matters are treated,— our lessons read in church too often are.

Now the offices in our Prayer-Book are, as has been already said, for the most part made up out of the old Catholic offices, the common religious offices of Christendom before it was divided. But whoever looks at a Catholic service-book will find that the lessons there are in general very much shorter than ours. There are more of them and they are much shorter, aiming at being as far as possible, all of them, complete wholes in themselves, and at producing one distinct, powerful, total impression ; which is the right aim for lessons to follow. To this end chapters are broken up, and parts of them taken by themselves, and verses left out, and things which are naturally related brought together. And this not in the least with a controversial design, or to favour what are called Romish doctrines, but simply to produce a clearer and stronger impression. The unknown arranger of these old lessons has simply followed the instinct of a true critic, the promptings of a sound natural love for what is clear and impressive. And in following this, he

gives an instance of the truth of what I have somewhere
said, that practically, in many cases, Catholics are less
superstitious in their way of dealing with the Bible than
Protestants.

The fifteenth chapter of the First Epistle to the Corinthians appears in the Catholic offices for the dead,
but in detached portions ; each portion thus becoming
more intelligible, and producing a greater effect. Thus
the seven verses from the beginning of the 20th verse
(*Now is Christ risen from the dead*), to the end of the
26th (*The last enemy that shall be destroyed is death*),
form one lesson, and a most impressive one. Another
admirable and homogeneous lesson is given by taking the
verses from the 41st (*There is one glory of the sun*), to the
end of the 50th (*Neither doth corruption inherit incorruption*), then passing from thence to the beginning of
the 53rd (*For this corruptible must put on incorruption*),
and continuing down to the end of the next verse (*Death
is swallowed up in victory*). Here we have two separate
lessons, much shorter, even both of them together, than
the present lesson, and (I think it will be found) more
impressive by being detached from it.

But a lesson from the Old Testament is surely to be
desired also. Who would not love to hear, in such a
service, that magnificent prophecy on the breathing of

life into the dry bones, the first ten verses of the thirty-seventh chapter of Ezekiel? This also is to be found as one of the lessons in the Catholic offices for the dead. In the same offices is another lesson, even more desirable, it seems to me, to have in our burial-service ;— a lesson, the most explicit we have, a lesson from our Saviour himself on the resurrection of the dead. Simply that short passage of the fifth chapter of St. John, from the 24th verse to the end of the 29th ;—the passage containing the verse : *The hour is coming, and now is, when the dead shall hear the voice of the Son of God, and they that hear shall live.*

Thus we have, instead of one long and difficult lesson, four short, clear, and most powerfully impressive ones. Let the rubric before the existing lesson be changed to run as follows :—' Then shall be read one or more of these lessons following ; ' and we shall have the means of making time for the hymn, if hymns are desired, without unduly lengthening the service ; and if hymns are not desired, we shall be richer in our lessons than we are now.

But the hymn at the grave is not the only concession which we can without public detriment make in this matter to the Dissenters. Many Dissenters prefer to bury their dead in silence. Silent funerals are the practice in the Church of Scotland, and, I believe, with Presbyterians generally. To silent funerals in the parish churchyard there can manifestly be, on the score of order, propriety, and dignity, no objection. A clergyman cannot feel himself aggrieved at having to perform them. The public cannot feel aggrieved by their being performed in a place of solemn and public character. Whenever, therefore, it is desired that burial in the parish churchyard should take place in silence, the clergyman should be authorised and directed to comply with this desire.

4.

Thus I have sought to make clear and to justify what I meant by that short sentence about burials which occurred in what I said at Sion College, and at which a certain dissatisfaction was expressed by some whom I am loth to dissatisfy. The precise amount of change recommended, and the reasons for making it, and for not making it greater, have now been fully stated. To sum up the changes recommended, they are as follows :—The first rubric to be expunged ; four lessons to be substituted for the present single lesson, and the rubric preceding it to run : 'Then shall be read one or more of these lessons following ;' the words, *as our hope is this our brother doth*, to be left out ; a hymn or hymns, from one

of the collections in general use, to be sung at the grave
if the friends of the deceased wish it, and if they notify
their desire to the clergyman beforehand ; silent burial
to be performed on the like conditions.

The Dissenters, some of them, demand a great deal
more than this, and their political friends try to get a
great deal more for them.   What I have endeavoured is
to find out what to a fair and sensible man, without any
political and partisan bias whatever, honestly taking the
circumstances of our country into account and the best
way of settling this vexed question of burials,—to find out
what to such a man would seem to be reasonable and
expedient.   Nor are the concessions and changes proposed
so insignificant.   I believe the majority of the Dissenters
themselves would be satisfied with them.   Certainly this
would be the case if we count the Methodists with the
Dissenters, and do not mean by Dissenters, as people
sometimes mean, the political Dissenters only.   And those
who are incensed with the folly of some of the clergy in
this matter, and desire to punish them, would probably
find that they could inflict upon these men of arbitrary
temper no severer punishment, than by simply taking away
from them, where burials are concerned, the scope for exercising it.   However, my object in what I have proposed
is not to punish certain of the clergy, any more than to

mortify certain of the Dissenters, but simply to arrive at
what is most for the good and for the dignity of the
whole community. Certainly it is postulated that to
accept some public form shall be the condition for using
public and venerable places. But really this must be
clear, one would think, to any one but a partisan, if he
at all knows what 'things lovely and of good report' are,
and the value of them. It must be clear to many of the
warmest adversaries of the Church. It is not hidden, I
am sure, from Mr. John Morley himself, who is a lover
of culture, and of elevation, and of beauty, and of
human dignity. I am sure he feels, that what is here
proposed is more reasonable and desirable than what his
Dissenting friends demand. *Scio, rex Agrippa, quia
credis.* He is keeping company with his Festus Chamberlain, and his Drusilla Collings, and cannot openly
avow the truth ; but in his heart he consents to it.

And now I do really take leave of the question of
Church and Dissent, as I promised. Whether the
Dissenters will believe it or not, my wish to reconcile
them with the Church is from no desire to give their
adversaries a victory and them a defeat, but from the
conviction that they are on a false line ; from sorrow at
seeing their fine qualities and energies thrown away, from
hope of signal good to this whole nation if they can be

turned to better account. 'The dissidence of Dissent, and the Protestantism of the Protestant religion,' have some of mankind's deepest and truest instincts against them, and cannot finally prevail. If they prevail for a time, that is only a temporary stage in man's history ; they will fail in the end, and will have to confess it.

It is said, and on what seems good authority, that already in America, that Paradise of the sects, there are signs of reaction, and that the multitude of sects there begin to tend to agglomerate themselves into two or three great bodies. It is said, too, that whereas the Church of Rome, in the first year of the present century, had but one in two hundred of the population of the United States, it has now one in six or seven. This at any rate is certain, that the great and sure gainer by the dissidence of Dissent and the Protestantism of the Protestant re-ligion is the Church of Rome. Unity and continuity in public religious worship are a need of human nature, an eternal aspiration of Christendom ; but unity and con-tinuity in religious worship joined with perfect mental sanity and freedom. A Catholic Church transformed is, I believe, the Church of the future. But what the Dis-senters, by their false aims and misused powers, at present effect, is to extend and prolong the reign of a Catholic Church *un*transformed, with all its conflicts, impossibilities, miseries. That, however, is what the Dissenters, in their present state, cannot and will not see. For the growth of insight to recognise it, one must rely, both among the Dissenters themselves and in the nation which has to judge their aims and proceedings, on the help of time and progress ;—time and progress, in alliance with *the ancient and inbred integrity, piety, good nature, and good humour of the English people.*

LONDON : PRINTED BY
SPOTTISWOODE AND CO., NEW-STREET SQUARE
AND PARLIAMENT STREET

www.ingramcontent.com/pod-product-compliance
Lightning Source LLC
Chambersburg PA
CBHW020846270326
41928CB00006B/570

* 9 7 8 3 7 4 3 3 0 1 3 4 4 *